# Kitchen Party

# Kitchen Party
## Food Stories from Nova Scotia and Beyond

**Sheryl Kirby**

**illustrations by Katherine Verhoeven**

Published in Canada by Stained Pages Press
Toronto, Canada
www.stainedpagespress.com



Illustrations by Katherine Verhoeven



ISBN 978-0-9917377-0-3

To Helen Kirby, who may not love cooking,
but who surely made it fun and inspirational
for the rest of us.

# Contents

## Part 3 – Food Writing

# Introduction: The Kitchen Party

The down east "kitchen party" is usually not a planned event. No one invites you specifically to come and hang out in their kitchen. Rather, the kitchen party is the result of evolution.

In the small homes of blue collar families in the Atlantic provinces of Canada, the kitchen was by default often the biggest and warmest room in the house because that's where the bulk of the cooking and housework was done on a daily basis. Bedrooms needed only to fit a bed and a dresser. Living rooms or parlours tended to be used only on special occasions, and were generally decorated in a stiff and formal style; in the winter months, they could even remain cold to save on heating fuel.

So while someone might plan on hosting a party with the assumption that it would fill most of the public rooms of their house, inevitably, all of the fun seemed to take place in the kitchen.

There are other reasons for this phenomenon besides the innately practical, of course. It's almost a cliché to say that the kitchen is the heart of the home, but it's usually where the majority of Maritimers feel the most comfortable. Sitting around the kitchen table is where we eat our meals, where most of our discussions take place, where homework or board games or jigsaw puzzles are laid out on cold winter nights. It's where we spread paper to wrap Christmas presents, where we roll out fabric to sew a new dress, where school science fair projects come to life.

It's all well and good to hand a Maritimer a cocktail or a glass of wine and direct us to sit on your lovely sofa. We'll do so to be courteous, and we'll sit nicely in the polite manner our parents taught us. But we won't be comfortable, really. We'll be worried about spilling something, or letting our snarky down east sense of humour get the better of us and saying something inappropriate. But hand us a beer or a cup of rotgut orange pekoe tea and tell us to grab a seat at the kitchen table, then we'll be in our element.

This gathering around the table, whether an intentionally planned party complete with invitations, or an impromptu gathering that takes on a life of its own, is where Maritimers are happiest. Throw in some music (ideally live), some good food (ideally cooked while the party is going on), maybe some dancing if there's room, and something to drink (ideally alcoholic), and we're happy as clams. By the way, throw in a big pot of clams, too.

Be warned – kitchen parties can get raucous. While Maritimers are honest, hard-working people, few of us are genteel. Drinks will be spilled, arguments will be had, someone will likely try to do a crazy dance move and fall ass over teakettle. The table will be scarred with cigarette burns the next morning; empty beer bottles with be discovered in odd corners; hats, car keys and possibly underwear will be left behind inadvertently. There will be, have no doubt about this, hangovers.

And while this collection of stories and essays isn't specifically about kitchen parties in the traditional sense, I chose the title both as a nod to my Nova Scotian heritage, and as a representation of the coming together of food, family and friends. The same kitchens where my family partied and celebrated, where we talked and laughed, where we fought and cried, were the same rooms where I learned to cook. The kitchen is where I watched my grandmother turn out a perfect pie crust, and where we gathered around pots of mussels and periwinkles we had collected from the rocks of the nearby harbour. It's where I learned to make bread and doughnuts, and where we chopped onions wearing scuba goggles. The table where we feted my grandmother on her birthday with a custom-made cake decorated like balls of yarn to honour her love of knitting was the same one where she set out a cup of tea and a plate of cookies for her deceased husband every afternoon for nearly a year after he had passed away.

The best parties, and the best memories, are in the kitchen.

These stories and articles were created over the past decade, originally with the intention of entertaining friends on social media sites or my own blog, and then professionally via TasteTO, a website about food and drink in Toronto that I ran with my husband, Greg Clow, from 2007 to 2011.

They are arranged in an order that I refer to as "roughly chronological" based on when the story took place as opposed to when I originally wrote it, and are divided (again, roughly) into three sections that represent growing up in Halifax, discovering a world of cuisine upon moving to Toronto, and finally, developing the (hopefully) evolved palate and knowledge of a professional food writer trying to share experiences about food culture on a wider scale.

Upon selecting works for this collection, I tried not to muck about with the old stuff too much. Most writers are their own worst critics, and while I did rework many pieces for flow and context, I intentionally left some of the stories in their original rough state because over-editing them would have felt dishonest. Besides the evolution of my food knowledge and life experience, in many ways these stories reveal my growth and maturity as a writer.

So please, come on in, pull up a chair, let me pour you a drink, and fill your boots with stories of food, cooks, kitchens, and parties.

# Kitchen Party

# Part 1 - Nova Scotia

Kitchen Party

# King of Fish

MAAAACKrel! MAAAACKrel! MAAAACKrel!

As a small child I was fascinated with mimicking the mackerel man. We lived in a suburb of Halifax that verged on rural and some of the small fishing villages that dot the Nova Scotia coast were only a few miles away. While most of the Atlantic fishery is based on massive ships that travel far out to sea for days or weeks on end, the area around Halifax Harbour abounds with fish as well, and during mackerel season in the 1970s, a small-scale fisherman with a single boat could make a regular week's wages in one day simply by heading out to the mouth of the harbour in the morning to catch mackerel and then driving through the residential neighbourhoods at mid-afternoon, selling them from the back of his car or truck – just in time for supper. (This practice is not exclusive to fish, although the mackerel man is the most memorable. It is still not uncommon to buy strawberries, corn, or even lobster from the back of someone's car in suburban Nova Scotia.)

The mackerel man who frequented my grandmother's neighbourhood had a distinctive nasally voice and during the last weeks of June – when the mackerel started "running" – I would wait impatiently for his wood-panelled station wagon to make its way slowly up the street. I would then run out to greet the mackerel man, following along behind him, yelling "Mackerel!" at the top of my small lungs until we got to the point on the street where I was not permitted to go beyond by myself. Then the mackerel man would wave good-bye, and I would make my way home, continuing to yell "Mackerel!" until my grandmother stuck her head out the window, demanding that I shut the hell up.

In high school, the student body was comprised almost equally of both suburban students and kids from the rural fishing villages who were bussed in. In my senior year, only two weeks before final exams and graduation, every boy in my math class quit school to join their fathers on their boats. The mackerel were running and the mackerel don't wait. The teacher, aghast at the situation, pleaded with them to stay until graduation, but her request fell on deaf ears. "I don't need to graduate, Miss," was the reply, "I'm going to be a fisherman just like my Dad." This was, in retrospect, a profoundly short-sighted decision and no doubt all of those young men had to go back and re-do those courses to graduate once the Atlantic fish stocks took a turn for the worse. It goes to show, however, that in Nova Scotia, fish is still king, and the king of fish, for the small fisherman, is mackerel.

I haven't eaten mackerel in years. The last time was on a visit home when I joined my father and one of his friends on a evening boat ride to the mouth of Halifax Harbour where we used "trawling lines" (basically a fishing rod where the line is dragged slowly behind the boat) to catch a dozen or so fat, shiny mackerel. We cleaned them right on the boat, dumping the chum over the side for other fish to feed on. Then we brought them home, fried them up in a bit of butter, and were ever so pleased with ourselves.

That was probably about 10 years ago, and I had had a bad craving for mackerel for some time. It's almost impossible to find in Toronto, however. Even during mackerel season, most of the Atlantic catch doesn't make it this far, as it's not an especially popular fish outside of the Maritimes… and Portugal.

Fast forward to our recent house move, which now has us shopping at a supermarket in an area heavily populated with Portuguese families. We had been excited about the fish counter at this supermarket, but as we stood there yesterday, trying to decide between mussels and clams, Greg elbowed me. "What's Cavala?" he asked. "It sort of looks like mackerel, doesn't it?"

Yep, it does. That's because it is mackerel… in Portuguese.

Right there in front of me, mackerel. Now, it wasn't from Nova Scotia, which made me suspicious of the freshness. I asked to see it. The man behind the counter held up a fish and was surprised when I took it in my bare hands and sniffed it, then poked it, then stared into its eyes. I handed it back and smelled my hands – no fishy smell. Two big ones, please. Not as fresh as the ones we had caught and cleaned and feasted on all within a matter of hours, but still, mackerel.

We brought them home and I called my Dad. "Where the hell did you get mackerel in Toronto when I can't even get it here?" he demanded to know. "Portugal," was my smug reply, although Florida is a more likely guess. We discussed cooking options. While I love fried mackerel, I opted for broiling just because there would be less stink – the high oil content in mackerel makes for lots of smoke and stink. I coated the skin in a lime and garlic mustard and served it up with an organic green salad and roasted potatoes. It was perfect.

As long as the supermarket keeps it in stock, we will be eating mackerel on a much more regular basis (more regular than once a decade, at least!). It's an inexpensive fish, full of Omega 3 and B12, and is super delicious. I wonder, though, how the supermarket fishmonger would feel about me standing beside him yelling "MAAAAckrel!" at the top of my lungs.

# The Milkman

It's probably not a good thing to admit, but I am old enough to remember when milk was delivered to the door in glass bottles. At my Nanny Smith's house (she being my mother's mother) where I spent my school year weekdays as a child, the milkman would arrive in the morning and leave two bottles of milk at the foot of the stairs, just inside the back door. Presumably the door was left unlocked to allow him access, which seems like an odd thing to do now, but it was a different time back then, and people were more trusting, I suppose.

Unless it was a payment collection day, the milkman would leave the bottles and head back out to his truck, honking as he drove away, to let my grandmother know the milk was there. When I was old enough to be trusted not to drop the things, I was permitted to go down the stairs and bring each bottle, one at a time, up to the kitchen. It was there that my grandmother would take the tip of a paring knife to remove the paper cap, embossed with the Farmer's Dairy logo, and pour off the thick, slightly yellow cream. I recall not liking this especially when offered some, it being too thick and cloying and tasting oddly of grass as opposed to sweet like the vanilla ice cream I was expecting.

The switch to cardboard cartons must have happened at some point during my youth because I can remember carrying these up the stairs as well, a bright red half-gallon carton full of homogenized milk and a smaller carton of cream, the existence of which my grandmother bemoaned – she had been a great fan of the glass bottles.

Technology, however, had moved her milk delivery into the future. Those old glass bottles were dangerously slippery in the hand, and the milk stayed fresher when not exposed to light. And the advancements in homogenization meant that the dairy could sell a consistent product.

Since both my parents worked, we never had our milk delivered, but the milkman was a regular part of my other grandmother's day as well. She was usually home, so the milk man would knock on the door and hand her the order. And while my Nanny Smith only ever got those two bottles of cream-topped milk, at Nanny Kirby's house, where she always had a houseful of kids and grandkids to feed, the delivery was more along the lines of four cartons of milk, a couple of quarts of a juice drink called Beep! for us to drink with our lunch, and in the early 1970s, single-serving bags of juice that were pierced with a straw.

The precursor to the modern juice box, these juice bags held about 8 ounces of various, not especially healthy juices in flavours like grape, orange and tropical (I recall one tasting like Tahiti Treat). The idea was that you took the accompanying straw that had a pointy end and pierced the bag in a spot along the seam across the middle.

My Grandmother Kirby lived at the top of a street called Mountain Road. It was the highest point in the city and you could stand in the front yard and look out over Halifax Harbour. In the summer of 1973, the City of Halifax was finally getting around to servicing Mountain Road with water and sewage – up until that time, my grandparents sourced their water from a well in the front yard and used an outhouse in the back. In Nova Scotia, which is mostly one huge chunk of granite, the process of laying sewer pipes involved massive quantities of dynamite and huge buffer pads made of old tires to keep the exploded bits of granite from flying around like shrapnel.

That summer, my cousin Kenny and I spent every day sitting on my grandparents' front steps, watching the progress of the work crews as they blasted open the street and laid the pipes that would make our grandmother's household life a thousand times easier. As someone who had lived most of her life without running water, my grandmother was delighted with the final results. To this day I have never seen someone turn on a tap with so much complete and utter joy.

Across this labyrinth of boards and piles of pipes and stacks of dynamite that made the street look like a Wile E. Coyote cartoon, the milkman made his way to the back door each day, the box of milk cartons, juice cartons, and wacky juice bags teetering precariously as he tried to keep his balance.

Kenny and I would wait impatiently for the bags of juice to get cold, and then we'd make our way to the front steps – either down the driveway and through the hedge of fragrant wild rose bushes (watch out for the bees!) or, when the workmen were laying pipes in the driveway, through the living room and the weird little front storm porch that was only ever opened in the summer to allow a breeze into the house.

There we'd quickly suck dry the bags of juice, creating an odd strangling sound as the plastic contracted with our inhaled breath, and then we'd exhale into the empty bags until they were full of air and we found ourselves in varying states of dizziness. Then, ever so carefully, we'd pierce the other side of the thick plastic with the pointy end of the straw. If we did this right, we were left with a pierced balloon, still full of air.

Then we waited.

As the work crews readied the dynamite and backhoes lifted the huge pads into place to absorb the shock of the blast, we'd place our air-filled juice bags on the ground. When the loud horn blast sounded to warn of the impending explosion, we'd stand on one leg, the alternate foot hovering in the air above the bags. And then, when the dynamite exploded and the blast shook the house and the ground, and the smell of spent dynamite filled the air, we'd stomp on our juice bags, causing what were really sad little bangs compared to the deafening boom we were trying to match.

Then we'd run back into the house and ask for another.

Eventually, my grandmother caught on to our scheme. It might have been that we got impatient waiting for the crews to blast more dynamite and just started exploding the bags at will. It might also have been that the milkman, who had once witnessed our trick, ratted us out. Or it might have been that we went through so much juice that summer that my grandmother feared for both our teeth and her grocery budget and put a stop to it all.

Like the old glass bottles, the bags of juice were eventually deemed unsafe (dire stories of children exploding full bags and sending pointy straws flying too close to little faces made the rounds at school) and the following summer, with no construction crews and no exploding juice bags, we were left to find other, less interesting pursuits.

# Mornings Over a Hot Stove

My Grandmother Kirby's birthday was yesterday, and I finally remembered to call her – this morning. It turned out for the best, actually; she had so many people calling her last night that I probably wouldn't have been able to get through. Calling today, I got to talk to her for almost an hour.

She was delighted that my uncle had taken her out for Chinese food, one of her favourite treats ever. Chinese food to my grandma is chicken balls in Jell-O, and I have my doubts that she'd care for real Chinese food very much at all, but it's the closest she's going to get in Halifax, so there's no real basis for comparison.

Besides the fact that she just loves to eat Chinese food, my grandmother remarked that it's also a nice treat because she doesn't have to cook. "Damn, I hate cooking!" she exclaimed.

This statement took my world and turned it upside down, and shook the shit out of it. I had to ask her to repeat herself, something that she usually has to do with me, especially when she's not wearing her hearing aid.

"Oh, no, I hate cooking with a passion. I like baking okay, that's alright. But I've been cooking since I was nine years old. I've HAD to cook since I was married, and I can't tell you how much I hate it!"

This revelation was akin to hearing Wayne Gretzky say that, yeah, hockey is an okay game, but he really wishes he had taken up soccer instead. Or David Bowie stating that he sings because he can but he would be happier if he had become a bricklayer. See, grandmother = food = love. My grandmother taught me to cook; she made it fun, interesting, enjoyable. She's the one who really sparked my passion for food and cooking. I guess I never really realized that part of her goal in making the process fun was a selfish one, a way to make a tedious, hated chore marginally enjoyable for her as well.

Thinking about it, I can see how she would feel that way – three meals a day, for more than seventy-five years now. At age nine, she took on partial responsibility for preparing her family's meals. She was the youngest; most of her older siblings had married and moved out, but there were always people to be fed. Living on a farm during the Depression, everyone had to pitch in, and her job was to help cook.

Ten years later, she was married and had a husband to cook for. My grandfather was definitely one of those men who demanded a hot meal three times a day, and it was my grandmother's job as the housewife to prepare those meals. During the years that my grandfather drove a cab, that meant getting up at 4am to cook him breakfast. No cereal or toast, either – there had to be meat, usually bacon or a piece of trout, eggs, pancakes, coffee. All this prepared on a big old kerosene stove that needed about 30 minutes to get hot enough to cook on.

My grandfather also refused to eat store-bought bread, which left my grandmother with the task of baking bread two or three times a week, even in the sweltering heat of summer. There also always had to be dessert with supper, although the wonders of the modern age provided her with instant puddings, Jell-O, and packaged cake mixes to make her life a tiny bit easier.

Then there were the rest of us to look after. With four sons and no daughters of her own, my grandmother got stuck with the job of cooking for everyone, with no one available to help her in the least. With four grandkids to trip over in her small kitchen, plus her two sons still at home, she was like a personal chef to each and every one of us. Our grapefruit was sectioned, our cheese and crackers lightly buttered to keep them from falling apart, our pancakes shaped like our initials, and my Uncle Al got his morning eggs served up in an ice cream sundae dish with toast soldiers sticking out of the top. She took full advantage of frozen french fries and pizzas, store-bought cupcakes and other convenience foods when she could, but mostly she cooked for us, and she did so without complaint.

Knowing more now about what her life was like than I did as a child, I can see that she really had no other choice. That's what a housewife did – she took care of her family, no matter how difficult it might be, no matter what abuse might be heaped upon her. It was a generation that didn't complain; you made do and were happy for the little bit of pleasantness that life afforded you. It was a hard life, my grandmother's, but she never made it seem hard. She made it seem effortless and natural and fun. It's fun when you don't have to do it three times a day every day for decades, fun when you don't have to get up at 4am to light a stove, fun when you don't have to haul water from a well in order to wash the dishes.

It makes me feel kind of stupid, in a way. Not to have realized before this how hard her life must have been back in those days. I was a child, of course, but I know enough about history and social progress to know what drudgery most women experienced in past generations.

She was, IS, my inspiration. She is why I went to cooking school, why I dreamed of becoming a chef. Mind you, my original goal before the government slightly sidelined me, was baking and pastry, not straight-up "cooking," so maybe her attitude had more of an effect on me than I realize. The baking is the stuff that we were mostly allowed to help with, it was the stuff she really made fun. I don't, now that I think about it, recall doing a lot of meal preparation with my grandmother. She was happiest to just have the kitchen to herself without her brood underfoot – get it over with as quickly and easily as possible, I guess. Which is also like me; I prefer to cook alone. I enjoy it more than my grandmother, and I tend to find a zone or a groove that I'm betting she never achieved, but I'm better at it by myself than if I have help.

I'm glad that, now in her golden years, she doesn't have the same demands placed on her. She still cooks, and there are still mouths to feed (my Uncle Al still lives at home with her), but at least it's gotten easier. An electric stove, a microwave, running water. Not having to get up and cook a meal at 4 am must be something that she is thankful for every single day.

And Chinese food. Don't forget the Chinese take-away – she's mighty thankful for that, too.

# The Food Emporium

When I was a wee thing, one of my greatest delights was stopping at the bakery counter at Simpsons where my mother would buy me a gingerbread man. The bakery and candy counter at the Simpsons department store in Halifax was right by the main doors, which opened onto the city bus depot, making it convenient for anyone who had to switch buses to get to where they were going to grab a snack.

In those days, department stores stocked a huge variety of sweets, particularly penny candy, which made them a place of true wonderment for a kid. After perusing the aisles of mints and rainbow-coloured hard candy, I'd clutch my gingerbread man tightly all the way home, careful not to let an arm or leg break off before I could eat him.

At some point in my early teens, Simpsons moved to the other end of the mall, and Sears took over the space, removing the street-level candy and bakery counter and forcing a bit of a trek for anyone who wanted some candy, or a gingerbread man or a bag of Chinese chews for the bus ride home.

When I moved to Toronto in the late 1980s, the food emporium at Eaton's department store was a treasure trove of delights. Sure, I lived in Kensington Market and could have my pick of bizarre Asian fruit or Portuguese fish or real cream cheese, but the aisles of shortbread, jam and tea in the basement of Eaton's made me feel safe and happy in a city that was often foreign and scary to a teenager a thousand miles away from home. That it was full of sweet little Scottish grandmothers didn't hurt either.

Over the years the food emporiums of both the now-defunct Eaton's and The Bay (formerly Simpsons) at Yonge and Queen Streets have morphed with the times. When Sears took over the Eaton's space, the basement floor became part of the mall – if Sears has ever had a food section, I've never found it.

At The Bay, the food section still exists, but it shrinks every few years as the demand for high-end household goods grows. Five-hundred-dollar sets of pots turn a bigger profit than penny candy, which The Bay no longer carries. The bakery, once huge and offering customized cakes, is a mere counter, full of stuff prepared elsewhere, and the deli is one small section of a prepared-foods area that specializes in pizza and Caribbean cuisine. There was a big café there for a while, with plush comfy chairs, and at one point about 2000 square feet of interesting prepared items such as mustards, jams, preserves and bread.

It's not that people don't want these things anymore – fine food shops are springing up everywhere and luxury products are hugely popular. But department stores, especially those with aspirations of being high-end, would rather take up floor space with expensive items with a larger profit margin. So 600-thread-count sheets will always win out over candy. And even the candy that The Bay stocks is swank, with names like Godiva taking up most of the small area allotted to sweets.

Now that The Bay has been sold to a US chain, it will be interesting to see what changes occur. There's already talk of splitting up the historic building and cutting out certain merchandise segments to allow for higher-end items. Which makes me wonder if there will be room again for a food emporium.

Funnily enough, while walking through the small food area of The Bay the other day, I spied gingerbread men in the bakery case. As I bought one and prepared to stick the bag in my backpack, the sweet Jamaican lady behind the counter seemed distressed. "You'll break his arms off before you can eat them!" she said in that classic accent. "You don't want that!"

"You're right," I said, gently removing the brown paper bag from my pack. "I should be more careful."

I carried that bag separately the whole way home, despite having a backpack and an additional heavy bag. I resisted the urge to munch on my gingery friend on the streetcar, and was happy to see that he made it home to the plate in one piece, although he did lose one of his royal icing eyes in the process.

I wonder how long the little bakery counter will remain after the store officially changes hands; will they keep it or scrap it? I wonder if little kids today even care about gingerbread men. And I wonder where Scottish grandmothers go to buy their shortbread and jam now that Eaton's is a distant memory.

Certainly, you can't stop progress and things don't ever stay the same, but carrying home that gingerbread man made me so very happy. Happier than over-priced cupcakes or fancy restaurant meals ever have. I hope there's still a place for bakery counters and gingerbread men once the store is renovated. Treats from the department store food emporium are an integral part of childhood – it would be a shame to lose that.

Sheryl Kirby

# The Christmas Treats

When I was growing up, like any family, my family had snack foods in the house, and throughout the year, these were pretty basic: (mostly) homemade cookies, chips, ice cream. But at Christmas, the grocery cart would fill with more premium brands. To this day, it doesn't seem like the holidays to me without certain items: notably a can of Poppycock, a tin of Quality Street chocolates, Coca-Cola, and Bits and Bites. These were the more expensive versions of things we would otherwise buy, but probably because they were more expensive, they only showed up at our house in December. It got me thinking recently as to whether these items were really better than their rest-of-the-year counterparts, or whether the novelty of having them at holiday time simply made them seem better.

## Poppycock versus Cracker Jack

I can't find an ingredients list for either of these versions of candy/caramel corn, but I'm going to post one in the Poppycock column without too much debate. Freshness seems to be a key here, plus premium nuts as opposed to peanuts, but it's really the coating that wins it. Without seeing an ingredients list (and after coming across ingredients for some of the "Indulgence" varieties of Poppycock that include cottonseed oil, I'd rather not know what the stuff is made of, to tell the truth) it at least seems as if there's a more "buttery" flavour to the premium brand. Cracker Jack, on the other hand, although available year-round, is often stale and hard and cheap-tasting. Googling "Poppycock" actually gave me a number of recipes, so I might try to appease my urges this season with some homemade stuff instead.

## Coca-Cola versus Pop Shoppe

In the past few years, someone has revived and rebranded Pop Shoppe pop as a high-end product, but back in the 1970s and 1980s, it was the cheapest of the cheap soda, available in a rainbow of flavours for literally pennies a bottle. I drank a lot of lime rickey, cream soda and root beer as a kid, while my parents suffered the subsequent dental bills to vouch for my efforts. During the holidays, though, there was always a bottle of Coke in the fridge. This was less as a treat for us kids than it was a mix offering for guests drinking the ubiquitous downeast rum and Cokes, but we always managed a glass or two before the bottle was gone.

## Bits and Bites

I have no idea why I associate this product with the holidays, and back in my childhood, there wasn't the alternative General Mills version available. And despite hating the little cheese sticks with a passion (still do), I always get a craving for this snack when Christmas rolls around.

## Quality Street Chocolates

It's not that we had chocolates in the house all the time, and our family always had a habit of sticking with a box of good old Halifax-made Pot of Gold come Christmastime. But because they were considered "fancy", someone always bought my grandmother a big honkin' tin of Quality Street for Christmas. And I mean the biiiig tin – like, 5 pounds at least. On Christmas Day, siblings and cousins jostled for a seat as close to the crystal candy dish as possible, waiting and fidgeting until we were offered one of Nanny Smith's special chocolates. The braver ones (or more fool-hardy – or more sugar-obsessed) would sneak an extra one or two, but only if they had been smart enough to wear something with pockets so they could hide the extra wrappers.

## Voortman Cookies

Admittedly, I still buy these cookies, although only at Christmas. I feel less guilty about it now that they're trans-fat free. This tradition came from my Grandmother Kirby, who had a pile of kids and grandkids to feed out of a tiny kitchen with a kerosene stove. The rest of the year we had either homemade cookies or typical store-bought brands like Oreos or Pirate cookies, but I waited for Christmas and those almonette cookies, all doused up with fake almond flavouring and dusted with powdered sugar that left a trail down my shirt and throughout the house. Fortunately, my husband had a Voortman cookie childhood too, so he's always happy when December hits and I bring home the Voortman cookies – still two packs for $2.50.

## Cranberry Jelly from a Can

Since I've lived on my own I've always made my own cranberry jelly, but growing up, we had the stuff from the can. My father didn't like the chunky version, and the concept of cheesecloth and straining a jelly seems not to have been invented at that point in history, so the can always made an appearance at Thanksgiving and Christmas. My mother wouldn't just open the can and spoon it into a dish, though. She would open both ends and, leaving one lid covering the jelly, would push the contents out the other end – and slice it! Thus, cranberry jelly appeared on our plates as a round red disc, jiggling heartily as we all cut our meat. My homemade cranberry jelly, made with orange rind and a touch of clove, tastes far better than the canned stuff, but sometimes, I miss the jiggle.

I'm sure there are more things that I could dredge up, but I'm not sure my brain can manage a craving for one more thing right now. As we've gotten older, my husband and I have created our own holiday traditions, and most of the ones described above have not survived. Mostly. Certainly neither of us would complain if a can of Poppycock or a tin of Quality Street showed up under the tree this year.

# The Big Black Stove

My Grandmother Kirby's stove wasn't completely black. While it had a black flat-top that had to be regularly scrubbed and blacked with some sort of paint-like stuff that came in a tube, the sides were shiny white and the fixtures were spring handles, all made from that gloriously reflective steel. But when I remember it, I mostly remember the top, and think of it as a black behemoth.

Until about 1980, my grandparents lived in a little four-room house atop a hill that overlooked Halifax Harbour. The massive stove that dominated their kitchen ran on a combination of wood and kerosene and was the main source of heat throughout the year, with a smaller kerosene-only stove set up in the living room during the winter months as an auxiliary supply.

Most days, the kitchen stove was fired up from the early morning until late evening, my grandmother churning out breakfast, lunch, and dinner to feed her immediate family (herself, my grandfather, and two sons still at home), plus an assortment of grandkids and in-laws who wandered in and out through the course of the day.

From an early age, my cousin Kenny and I were taught to fear and respect that stove. Because it was almost always running, it was always hot, especially the top. You walked past it carefully, keeping your hands to yourself, and you always, always used a pot holder to grab the shiny spring-like handles on the doors. Being the little shitheads that we were, we once indulged in a great game of wetting our hands and flicking the water onto the hot stove top, watching it bead and sizzle and skitter across the flat black burner plates. This got us a stern talking to for playing around something that was not a toy. We weren't hurting anything really, but the idea of respecting something that was potentially dangerous was definitely drilled into our heads.

When we were well behaved, we were allowed to help at the stove. A chair would be pulled up for us to take turns standing on and we were allowed to watch as rounds of nutmeg-spiced dough were added to a huge pot of boiling hot fat and puffed up golden brown to be the best doughnuts ever. As we got older and had proven that we could be careful, we were each allowed to take the long-handled metal spoon and dip it into that hot oil and flip those same doughnuts over to cook on the opposite side, a task that we did not take lightly, often arguing about whose turn it was and how long the other had been standing on the chair, but never ever pushing or fussing too much, lest the privilege be revoked.

On mornings when my grandmother made me pancakes for breakfast, I was allowed back up on the same chair to watch as she poured the batter into shapes and squiggles: Mickey Mouse, my initials, attempts at something that was supposed to be a cat.

In the summer months, we fled from the stove and the heat it generated, outside to the fresh Nova Scotian air. Being in that kitchen was often unbearable and my grandmother would lead us on hikes through the woods to search for berries or mushrooms or simply to take a dip in a nearby lake, anything to get away from the stifling heat of that little house. We'd return in time for her to watch her TV "stories" and to pull loaves of fresh bread from the oven. As soon as the bread was cool enough to cut, my grandmother would give Kenny and I each a heel slathered with butter and drizzled with thick dark molasses, and we would sit on the back porch, our beach towels spread underneath us, flip-flops and sneakers kicked off, and enjoy our favourite treat.

In winter, when the wind and snow howled around that little house, the seat at the table closest to the stove was a most coveted spot, and our playtime often involved table-top pastimes like games and puzzles and crafts which allowed us to sit in the warm kitchen instead of in the colder living room. We'd take an old camp blanket and some extra chairs and make a tent, getting it as close to the stove as we could without the risk of getting yelled at for not being careful. Despite the more liberal attitudes of the time regarding what children were allowed to do in terms of chores and dangerous tasks, someone was always afraid that we'd set ourselves on fire.

In fact, the only fire that ever occurred was one evening when the chimney got blocked. The house quickly filled with an acrid black smoke – kerosene has a particular toxic stink to it – and my grandmother had my Uncle Al take us down the street to my cousin Kenny's house. We were all frightened but when we came into the kitchen of the small apartment to discover my father and my Uncle Kenny with a huge pot of steamed clams, the fear and worry soon evaporated. By the time the clams were gone, we had the all-clear to return, and while I was quite young at the time, I can still remember the firemen stomping through my grandmother's house in their big coats and boots, and the concern on her face at the stench of smoke and the huge sooty marks on her wall.

Being a farmer's daughter and not especially well-off, it was par for the course that my grandmother would put up preserves every summer. I seem to recall some work-sharing and co-operation with regard to the putting by. Aunt Barb, Kenny's mother, would make bread and butter pickles; my mom would make chow chow; and my grandmother would make tomato chutney, all of which would be shared amongst the family. These were mostly solitary endeavours, each woman working alone in her own kitchen, but one year, for some reason – maybe it was the year my grandmother had fallen on an icy sidewalk outside the grocery store and broken her hip – all the women of the family were present to help with the chutney.

My job was to stand on that same old vinyl chair (retro furniture shops and restorers call it "cracked ice vinyl", and man, it isn't cheap nowadays) with the chrome legs, and watch the tomatoes in the pot of boiling water. When the slits that had been made in the skin opened and expanded, I took a slotted spoon and lifted them out into a waiting bowl of cold water. Then Aunt Barb would come and peel the things before passing them on to my mother to chop and seed.

What I also remember about my grandmother's stove is what she didn't cook on it. Michael Pollan, in his book In Defense of Food says "Don't eat anything your great-great-grandmother wouldn't recognize as food." When the book came out, people began shortening great-great-grandmother to just grandmother, and I remember railing against the mistake. My grandmother was a typical 1950s housewife – who happened not to have the modern conveniences most housewives had at the time. With no running water and no fancy electric range, daily meal preparation was a huge amount of work for her. Can anyone blame her for embracing canned, boxed, or otherwise prepared foods?

As kids, my cousins and I got frozen fries and frozen pizzas at lunch. We ate gelatin and pudding from a box. We ate cupcakes bought in a store. I'm not sure why I remember those cupcakes so well – they were all vanilla cake and came a dozen to a box and were arranged in three rows of four, each row with a different flavour of frosting (vanilla, strawberry or chocolate). In retrospect, I don't remember them being very good, and the frosting tasted vaguely of chemicals, but at the time, we loved the things. And for some reason, they've become a symbol of my grandmother's kitchen emancipation. When food elitists slam prepared food and I rush to the defence of women like my grandmother, who already had so much work to do everyday taking care of us all, those cupcakes are what always come to mind.

My grandmother, despite her professed dislike of cooking, was a wizard at that stove, turning out many meals for little money and ensuring that three generations of family members were happy and well fed on a daily basis. My inner elitist foodie doesn't feel angry or ashamed that she bought us store-made cupcakes on occasion to cut down on her workload. Rather, I'm happy and thankful that she took such good care of us, that she cared about our pleasure enough to buy us the occasional treat.

I assume the stove is long gone now. My grandparents moved out of that little house more than 30 years ago, and it's been renovated and retro-fitted a few times over. The last time I was in Halifax, I rode past it on the bus (such modern conveniences! In our day the bus stopped at the bottom of the hill and you had to walk the 15 minutes up the steep incline), and it was barely recognizable.

No doubt the old stove has long ago been relegated to the big scrap metal heap in the sky. But I can't help missing it sometimes. It's where my love of food and cooking developed, it's where I spent some of my favourite times as a child. And it is where my most vivid memories of my grandmother take place.

Last year, as I was getting my most recent tattoo, I looked up at the tattoo artist's work board of pieces in progress to see that he had created a beautiful rendering of a heart, kitted out to look like an old black stove, complete with ironwork handles and various doors and ovens on the ventricles. It was an original piece, envisioned and commissioned by another customer who happened to be a pastry chef, so asking him to tattoo it on me would have been akin to stealing. But as I stood there admiring it, I felt tears well up in my eyes. The stove, oh yes, the old black stove. It surely is the heart of the home.

# The Fake Shrimp

*And I'm the shrimp,*
*The smallest of all,*
*They call me the shrimp*
*Because I'm not very tall.*

Who knew that my theatrical claim to fame would be at the age of ten, singing a song about fish, and being photographed in a shrimp costume?

Our school, not having the money to pay for royalties for a more well-known Broadway-style musical, instead performed a creation called Time Fog, for our annual play, a historical tour of Nova Scotia, as written by the school's music teacher. It dealt with the expulsion of the Acadians, the founding of the City of Halifax, and even

Confederation. One scene explored Nova Scotia's rich fishing heritage.

I didn't play the Shrimp in the stage version, I was a mere extra, but the play had gotten such a huge amount of coverage in the local news that the school was asked to create a recording and slide presentation to send around to other schools. The kid who played Shrimp was sick on recording day, and as I was the first person in the line of sight of the music teacher (being able to fit into the shrimp costume didn't hurt) I was the lucky gal who got to wander through the school to the set, trying to keep the other kids from pulling off my many legs.

But I was, ultimately, the fake Shrimp. And the kid who brought the role to life onstage never let me forget it.

I was reminded of my Shrimp role recently when I picked up a package of soy-based shrimp at the local health food store. It doesn't actually say "shrimp" on the package anywhere, it's "Szechuan Style Stir-Fry", but what comes out of the little shrink-wrapped blob is definitely meant to look like shrimp.

Although I was pescetarian for many years, I stopped eating shrimp early on. After reading the works of Dr. Vandana Shiva about the destruction shrimp farming has caused in coastal India and Thailand, I couldn't justify it. I didn't like the things that much. In recent months, even Walmart has hopped on the sustainable shrimp bandwagon, and is supposedly refusing to sell any shrimp not farmed in a sustainable manner. Given that shrimp farming has been linked to the destruction caused by the 2004 tsunami, this is definitely a step in the right direction.

But back to my faux shrimp. The product is made by a company in Montreal, that is most well known for its seitan-based Smoked Wheat and Roast Wheat, pastrami and roast beef copies that are probably the most authentic faux meat products I've ever had. I figured the "stir-fry" would be good too.

The fake shrimp look like the real thing. Freakishly so. They're even pinkish on the outside to mimic the various sections of the tail. Taste-wise, shrimp tend to take on the flavour of what they're cooked in; on their own, they're pretty bland, so a soy copy works pretty much like all soy-based products do, sucking up the surrounding sauce. It was the texture that was so very wrong.

Shrimp is one of those meats with a bit of bounce. No matter how it's cooked, it's always slightly tough, with a bit of spring to it. My faux shrimp were doughy, almost fluffy, inside. It was sort of like eating a shrimp-shaped ball of bread.

As there were only six in the package, we managed to finish them, but afterwards, Greg and I looked at each other and admitted our buyer's remorse.

I don't know whatever happened to the kid who played Shrimp. I don't even remember his name. But somewhere out there, there are photos and recordings of me, pretending to be the Shrimp, and, like my soy-based shrimp product, probably doing a really bad job of it.

# Blueberries

I made The Grunt the other day. Or rather, I stewed the blueberries and then realized I was out of milk to make the dumplings. And then the kitchen got too hot and I was whingy and just jammed the pot, sans dumplings, into the fridge, where it took up too much space and sent the condiments jostling for elbow room. Finally this morning I made soft little biscuits and plopped them into the pot of boiling blueberry stew and watched them turn purple, then cobalt, as they puffed up with steam. Blueberry grunt is the ugliest food known to mankind (I'm purposely ignoring offal), but one of the best summer breakfasts ever.

In my constant complaining about the heat, there are a few things that I forget about which actually make August redeemable. Peaches and Cream corn with the silks still wet; muskmelons so strong that the smell begins to make you ill from its sweetness; baskets of small red plums, hot from the sun, with skin that cracks in your mouth, offering a warm, sugary burst as the flesh melts away from the stone. And, of course, blueberries.

I grew up in an area of Nova Scotia that was somewhere between suburban and rural. It was the city, but not quite. We had amenities, four-lane highways and fast-food restaurants, but you could walk out the back door into the trees and lose yourself in an area of forest about 15 miles square. Eventually, in any direction, you'd hit a highway, but it might take you a while, assuming you weren't travelling in circles.

Deep into these woods a mile or so was an area known as "the barrens". When I was seven there was a huge fire in the forest behind our house, and while it never came particularly close, we all had bags packed in case we were ordered to evacuate. My grandfather, who was a firefighter at the time, injured his knee rather severely fighting this blaze and had to have his kneecap removed, precipitating his eventual retirement. Besides the devastation it created for our family, the fire also tore through a few miles of trees, destroying everything in its path. A couple of years later, as burnt-out forests are wont to do, the area became overrun with blueberries.

We would go not with cups, but huge Tupperware containers big enough to hold a layer cake, or a big plastic washbasin, or even a large, clean bucket. We would fill them. Every time. Two, three, or four days in a row. We would pick and pick and pick until our fingers were stained purple and our arms were sunburned and our backs ached from being bent over the bushes and rocks for so long. Teeny tiny little wild blueberries, most no bigger than the nail on your baby finger, each picked carefully to avoid leaves and stems or the possibility of crushing the things.

Needless to say, I hated picking blueberries with a passion. I would make up any excuse I could think of to avoid the trek back into the thick woods and the subsequent hours of picking in the hot sun on that rocky open barren. I was bribed, cajoled, and ordered, I was threatened with being banned from eating any of them. Ultimately, my father was enlisted to force me out the door, and with my alternative being a smack upside the head, off I went, griping the whole way. It wasn't that my mother necessarily needed the extra berries my hands would pick.

To this day, I can't remember exactly what we did with the gallons upon gallons of berries we brought home. There was the grunt, of course, and some for pies and muffins, but it seems as if we must have picked a ton of the dusty little blue orbs each summer.

No, what my mother actually needed from me was my sense of direction. Never mind that from anywhere on the barren, which was up on a steep hill with large craggy granite boulders dotting the landscape, you could see the path that led to the road, or the lake in the other direction – she was terrified of getting lost in those woods, particularly in later years as the bushes and trees of the barren itself began to tower over her head. Once, she took a ball of yarn with her and laced it over branches to enable us to find our way back to the path. Then the yarn ran out and we continued to move away from it as we picked, and we eventually made our way down to the path the same way we did every time, with me pointing to the path below and plowing through the underbrush, a bucket of blueberries held aloft over my head to avoid spilling them. Everyone else would follow, in various degrees of consternation, trying to find a foothold and not drop their stash while keeping track of my orange bucket bobbing down the hill. I have no doubt that silly strand of red yarn is still there, and that the developers currently lobbying to turn my mother's beloved blueberry patch into shoddily built little townhouses will come across it when they eventually win the fight to break ground there.

Once home with our sapphire treasure, I was not free of the blueberry-related chores. They must be sorted and cleaned, then bagged and frozen. (No eating! You can eat them later when they're in the pie!) Once we were done, enough blueberries safely stored in the deep freeze to last us through the winter months, my mother would make the grunt. I never liked it much at the time even now I have a great aversion to soggy foods, and my mother's dumpling always came out on the wet side. But I would slurp at a small bowl of the hot cooked berries, soft and soupy and deeply purple, and let it be my reward for the mosquito bites, sunburned neck, and aching back I had acquired in the process.

It's been probably twenty years since I picked a blueberry off the bush and ate it in the hot sun, watching the horizon carefully for bears. My berries now come from the farmer's market or worse the supermarket. They're round and fat, some almost the size of grapes. They are sweet, of course, tasty, oh yes. But they'll never match the flavour of those tiny little wild berries snatched from my bucket on the walk home when I thought my mother wasn't watching.

# Those Who Like It, Like It a Lot

Even if it's not their beer of choice, it's impossible to find a Haligonian who doesn't know the name Alexander Keith. Besides having been the mayor of Halifax some three different times, Keith is most well known for his brewery, which was established in 1820 and still exists in downtown Halifax today, although the company itself is now owned by Labatt.

The stone building and courtyard (Keith was a high-ranking Freemason, so of course his entire complex was made of stone) is one of Halifax's main historic sites, and for years was home to a weekly Saturday morning farmers' market. (The farmers' market itself once doubled for a Connecticut-area market in a movie about Martha Stewart.)

One of the high-lights of any tour of the brewery is a stop at the tavern, where visitors can sample some of the various types of beer available under the Keith's brand. As a teenager, well before I and my high-school chums were even close to the age of majority, the tavern at the Keith's brewery, then known as Alexander's, was the one place in town where we knew we'd never get carded.

There we drank copious numbers of half-pint glasses of Keith's relatively low-alcohol beer, sprinkled lightly with salt, for something like 75 cents a glass. I can never remember any of us actually getting drunk. But the opportunity to go to a real bar, dance on the dance floor (albeit with kids from other high schools), and stay out late (or at least late enough – we all had a curfew) was exciting to a bunch of kids from the suburbs. Unlike a high-school dance, there was a decent sound system, no chaperones, and the opportunity to dance in a space that reeked of sophisticated smells like beer and cigarettes and too many types of bad cologne, as opposed to the school gym which always smelled of sweat socks.

When not sneaking into the bar at the Keith's brewery, I could often be found with a rowdier group of friends traipsing through Halifax's Camp Hill Cemetery, where Alexander Keith is buried. Labatt's current marketing team, intent on pushing Keith's as Nova Scotia's beer of choice (it wasn't in my day, and hopefully isn't now), makes a big deal of Keith's birthday, creating a whole urban myth about how Haligonians leave empty Keith's bottles and beer caps on the man's rather massive grave stone every October 5. (Again, let there be no doubt that the man was a Freemason and a pillar of Halifax society, because that's one huge gravestone.)

In fact, Keith's marker is the receptacle for empties and caps of all brands and varieties on most days of the year. For those of us who did the majority of our teenage drinking in the Camp Hill Cemetery, Keith's marker, prominent along the main pathway, was where we met with friends and started our evening, eventually moving away from the well-lit and well-trafficked area into the darker recesses of the graveyard, where we could drink in relative peace.

Despite having a husband who is a beer writer, it had actually been years since I'd had a Keith's, and while the brewery has offered a variety of beer styles over the years, it is most well known for the India Pale Ale.

A few years ago we attended an event here in Toronto: a pre-party a few weeks before Toronto's Festival of Beer. Sponsored by Keith's, it included a lobster supper and some Celtic music, plus some samples of Keith's IPA and the recently created Red.

When Greg placed the regular IPA in front of me, I sipped it and was confused. What was this? This was not the beer I remembered from my teenage years. This was not the beer in my glass all those nights at Alexander's, dancing to Duran Duran and sitting by the bar, where we were all fascinated by the rows of steaming hot and squeaky clean pint glasses emerging from the high-powered dishwasher.

As I've said, despite the huge marketing push, Keith's is not necessarily the favourite beer of Nova Scotians. Even back in the day, as an India Pale Ale it was considered extremely light, but I do recall it having flavour. The Keith's in front of me was like Bud Light. I sipped the sample of the Red and it was closer to what I remembered Keith's tasting like back in the 1980s.

It seems that the recipe for Keith's has changed significantly over the years, moving further and further away from the traditional proportions of what we consider an IPA.

India Pale Ale was created to be a hoppy beer, designed to survive long trips at sea, and to be refreshing to the British colonists in the hot climate of India. It is the current beer of choice for craft brewers who want to show off their crazy mad skills, and beers known as "hop bombs" are not uncommon as brewers add double or more the traditional amount of hops to create a unique and specialized drink.

In the 1800s, IPAs were highly hopped because the hops kept the beer from going off. Into the twentieth century, particularly as electric refrigeration became available, the proportion of hops decreased in the recipes at many breweries, likely because those old recipes were too bitter and hoppy for the average drinker, just as the hop bombs are today.

In 2010, Dalhousie University Archives in Halifax made public a variety of documents related to Keith's, as well as Oland, another local brewery. These documents included maps, letters and, most interestingly, recipe books, some of which clearly showed how the recipe for Alexander Keith's famous IPA had changed over the years. This information apparently caused some kerfuffle at Labatt, which owns both Keith's and Oland, and quickly forced Dalhousie to seal these records, claiming that they were actually the property of Labatt itself.

In the interim, Halifax indie weekly The Coast ran a piece by local drinks writer Craig Pinhey that detailed the changes in the IPA recipe over the years, specifically the decrease in the amount of hops from the 1910s to the 1940s and the introduction of corn sweetener and a further reduction of hops (from a proportion of 9000 pounds of malt and 160 pounds of hops in 1940 to 7300 pounds of malt, 1400 pounds of [corn] syrup and a mere 56 lbs of hops in 1971).

As was the case with Dalhousie, The Coast bowed to pressure by Labatt and pulled the piece from its website.

Keith's, and in turn Labatt, have made a big deal about the recipe remaining unchanged since 1820. Heck, in the 1970s and 1980s, it was the main gist of the brewery's ad campaign. Yet Pinhey includes the following passage in his piece:

> *I asked Graham Kendall, the current brewer of Keith's IPA, about these recipes in the context of modern brewing techniques. "As a brewer my job is to ensure that they get the same great tasting product that consumers appreciate time and time again," he answered. "I believe that the essential point is that beer lovers really aren't too hung up on the ingredients but rather the taste being what they expect."*

Which would be fine and true – if the taste of Keith's was, in fact, what was expected. My first taste of a Keith's after 15 years away from Halifax was most definitely not what I had expected. It was weaker, sickly sweet, watery and bland. It tasted nothing at all like what I remembered it to be.

I am not what is known as a "hop head" (a fan of the super-hoppy beers), but even I could have used more hops and less corn sweetener in my glass of Keith's. In the same way that I get cranky when a song from my youth, particularly something obscure and not of the mainstream, gets used in an ad for a car commercial, I was disappointed and annoyed that the Keith's available now doesn't taste the same way that it did in my youth. And remember that by the 1970s and 1980s, Keith's was already lower in hops and had corn sweeteners added to the mix. How much more has it been messed with it in the interim to make it more like those bland watery American beers?

Labatt may market the heck out of the tributes left at Alexander Keith's massive gravestone. The company may brand the outpouring as some kind of true Haligonian spirit and a respect for a product beloved over centuries (place your bets now on what kind of fuss will be rolled out in 2020 for the 200-year anniversary), but as a former Haligonian, I can vouch for two things: first, Keith's was never an outstanding beer, and second, it's now a shadow of its former self, especially in the taste department.

If you're in Halifax and happen to wander through Camp Hill Cemetery past Keith's resting place, don't bother to leave an empty or a bottle cap. If you're inclined to wrap the giant stone monument in hop vines, however, as decoration, or as a message to Labatt, there are many beer drinkers who would, as the old Keith's advertising slogan goes, like that a lot.

# Clam Digging

In the summer of 1986, I spent a weekend in Upper Economy, Nova Scotia. Upper Economy's claim to fame is that it is near the more populous town of Economy, where they have an annual clam festival. Located on the north eastern shore of the Bay of Fundy, Economy experiences the famous high tides of the region, with tides starting at 10 feet or more. At low tide, a person can walk out onto the sand flats for more than a mile.

These sand flats are mostly safe – Nova Scotia is a fairly solid hunk of granite with little topsoil, so deep quicksand, while it exists, is rare. What is plentiful in the miles of sparkling white sand are clams, and visitors to the area (the main industry appears to be cottages and campsites) can be found at low tide, buckets in hand, digging themselves up some supper.

Low tide is also a wonderful time for exploring the shoreline. Nearby Parrsboro is known for its amethyst deposits and when the tide is out, rocky outcroppings and caves appear, the walls of which can sparkle with the semi-precious gemstones. A caveat for explorers is to check your tidal charts; the Bay of Fundy tides come in faster than a man can run, and it's ever so easy to lose track of time while poking about in the caves, only to discover that you've got to climb a steep cliff face to escape drowning.

I was in Economy as the guest of my best friend, Toby, and her family. We were spending Labour Day weekend in her grandmother's cottage. Aunts and uncles also had cottages nearby and the weekend was to culminate in a huge lobster boil on the beach on Sunday night.

Our contribution to the dinner was to be clams. Clam digging is hard work – it's tough on the back, and there's often sunburn involved, and we weren't really looking forward to the chore. But as two oddly-dressed teenagers in a rural town of fifty people, we had exhausted our entertainment resources pretty quickly. So on the Sunday morning we donned our clam-digging gear, slathered our pasty goth skin in sunscreen, found some buckets and shovels, and headed out onto the sand flats.

When I say clam digging is hard work, I'm not kidding. The first step is to wander the sand flat, looking carefully for bubbles. The clam will bury itself in the sand a few inches down with its siphon just below the surface. As it expels water, small bubbles, similar to those in a pot of just-boiling water appear on the surface of the sand.

The digger then has to get their shovel into the sand a few inches away from the clam, very quickly force the shovel through the sand so that it's underneath the clam, and then scoop it up. If they're lucky, that scoop of heavy, wet sand will contain the clam they were digging for. More than likely, especially if the digger is inexperienced, the clam will have sensed the activity in the sand as soon as the digger touched down with their shovel, and will have forcefully propelled itself deeper down, leaving the digger with nothing but a shovel full of wet sand for their efforts.

It does get easier, but clam digging is also a task in which a digger can get so into what they're doing that they forget what's going on around them. Each clam in the bucket represents a small victory of man over beast, and the tendency to lose track of time is common.

After a couple of hours of digging on the sand flats that day, our buckets were each about half full. Not enough to feed the twenty or-so people who would be at the lobster boil, but a good start.

It was at that point when I thought to look up at the horizon, having heard something that sounded like crashing waves. The tide seemed to be a lot closer than it had been when we started.

"Uh, Toby," I asked with trepidation. "You checked the tidal charts this morning, right?"

"Yep," she replied, not looking up, her back to me and the incoming water.

"And you're sure the tide was going OUT when we started, right?"

Toby turned around. Squinting behind her purple-tinted sunglasses, she raised a hand to shade her eyes. Even today, more than a quarter century later, I can still see her standing there, black baggy pant legs rolled up, too-big striped t-shirt fluttering in the breeze, her pink, black and bleached blonde curls whipping around her face.

"Oh... shit. RUN!"

There was no mistaking it now, the tide was coming in, and it was coming in fast. Even worse, we had, without realizing it, wandered out onto the flats farther than we should have. By my calculation, we were about a quarter-mile out. We had a head start on the tide, which was still another half-mile or so behind us, but that wasn't much of a lead.

Neither Toby nor I was particularly sporty. Goths didn't do much running. And while I had some experience body-surfing on Nova Scotia's more sedate beaches, I knew that I'd not survive the pure power of the Bay of Fundy. Most people don't ever find themselves in a situation where they literally have to run for their lives, but that afternoon, that's exactly what we did.

Somehow we thought to grab the buckets of clams, although a couple of good shovels got left behind. The sand ahead of us up to the shore was now dry from the hot sun and was more difficult to run across in bare feet than if it had been wet. Thankfully, neither of us hit any quicksand. The last 50 yards or so before the shoreline were rock, and we stumbled across the smooth, rounded stones as the water hit us from behind with so much force that it nearly knocked us over.

The beach didn't transition to dry land smoothly, and the rocks stopped abruptly where the ground rose about 3 feet to the cottage's front lawn. This land would eventually wear away from the forces of waves and erosion, but for now, sandy soil made for a difficult climb.

We threw our buckets up onto to grassy edge of the lawn and clutched desperately to some well-rooted bushes as the water rushed up around our shoulders and one particularly large wave crashed over our heads. Toby climbed up first and then pulled me up, the two of us collapsing on the grass as the tide pounded angrily mere yards away.

A few minutes later, when our hearts had stopped beating so ferociously, we sat up and looked out over the water where huge waves swelled over the place we had been digging.

“I'm gonna get in shit for those shovels,” Toby said wryly.

“How did you misread the chart?” I asked as we crawled around picking up the clams that had flown from the buckets as we tossed them over the lawn's edge.

“I just checked the time of low tide. I guess I didn't check to see when it would be coming back in.” Typical Toby. I loved her like crazy, but she was always getting us into scrapes and near-death experiences like this.

Toby did get a talking to – not about the loss of the shovels but for putting us both in danger. At dinner that night, we were the talk of the party, especially when our meagre contribution had to be topped up by some clams purchased from a local fisherman, and the story of our sprint up the beach became part of Toby's family history.

But oh, I've never had a clam that tasted so good. Toby's uncles dug a huge pit and layered hot stones and piles of seaweed with our clams, some scallops, lobsters, and ears of corn. I think there might have been salads and rolls, but as we covered the many picnic tables with newspaper and set out bowls of melted butter, it was all about the food that came out of that pit.

We were exhausted, sunburned, and still suffering from a weird sense of shock from our brush with death, but when the piles of clams and lobsters were placed in front of us, did we ever eat. Butter dribbling onto our shirtfronts, all pretensions at being cool dropped away. We cracked open lobsters with our bare hands, sucked the juice from the shells of our hard-won clams, and listened to the waves crash nearby as the sun set and stars filled the late-summer sky, very, very thankful for our friendship, for the food before us, and for the fact that we were still there to enjoy it.

Sheryl Kirby

# Queen of Donairs

A couple of weeks ago, someone posted to the Toronto LiveJournal community, asking about where to get Nova Scotia-style donairs. After we collectively determined that there is no place in Toronto to get this much-loved street food, I fessed up and admitted that I have a copy of the original recipe created and marketed by the chain King of Donairs. And despite encouragement to start my own donair stand here in Toronto, I'd still rather just make the things at home.

While the donair resembles the traditional Greek gyro in many ways, it's not a gyro. Not even close. The meat is different and, more importantly, the sauce is different. How Halifax became the place where the gyro or doner kebab was bastardized and grew in popularity, I'll never know, but donair joints are on every block in downtown Halifax. Most of the shops that sell donairs also sell pizza, most famously on the corner of Blowers and Grafton Streets, or "Pizza

Corner", where three of the four corners (the fourth is a church) have some variation of a pizza/donair joint. There's even a donair pizza for those who can't decide.

It should be pointed out that Halifax has three different institutes of higher learning in its rather minuscule downtown area, which means a lot of students (note to anyone considering a trip to Nova Scotia, do not go to Halifax during the first few weeks of September – aka. frosh week), which means a lot of bars. At one point in the 1980s, Halifax had more bars per capita than any other city in North America. What this means is that there are a lot of drunk people looking for something to eat after last call.

And nothing is more satisfying than a donair.

It's hot, it's greasy, it's raunchy, it's sweet, and it's sticky. Some of my best memories of the summer of 1987 involve a walk through Victoria Park at 2am with my roommate Sharon, as we stumbled along, pissed off our asses, donair sauce running down our wrists and a chunk of hash in our pockets to smoke when we got home. Each time, it was the best donair ever.

When we moved to Toronto later that year, we discovered a donair shop in the food court at the Eaton Centre (back when the food court was near the centre fountain), but it disappeared after a bout of renovations.

Since then, I've been making my own. My mom used to work with the wife of the donair king and somehow scored the recipe. We made them all the time when I was a kid, and a phone call home got me a copy of the recipe so I could have donairs in Toronto. Going veg threw a bit of a wrench into my donair eating for a few years, but then one day I just craved the things so badly that I mashed some TVP together with the other ingredients and an egg and came up with something workable.

Addendum 2012 – In the years since 2006 when this piece was written, Toronto has been a wasteland for anyone searching for a good

Nova Scotia-style donair. A few places claimed to make an authentic version, but the donairs were either pre-made and reheated, or came with the garnishes more traditionally found on a Greek-style gyro.

Earlier this year, Toronto seemed to finally discover the authentic donair. Chef Geoff Hopgood opened Hopgood's Foodliner in the west end of the city, where he serves up a menu of Nova Scotia delicacies, including a smaller version of a real donair, along with dishes such as the traditional boiled dinner, and his mother's crab dip. In the west end, The Fuzzbox opened on Danforth Avenue, offering all of the delights available at Pizza Corner, from real donairs to donair pizza, and fried pepperoni.

Sadly, after speculation that donairs would be the next big food trend, the buzz seems to have died down. People don't really "get" the donair. Used to the savoury, yogurt-based sauce used on gyros, they find the sugary sauce of the donair (made with evaporated milk, sugar, garlic powder and vinegar) too sweet and sickly. Their palates are unable to appreciate the combination of sweet sauce and spicy meat. I have witnessed hard-core "foodies", people who will try anything, including anuses and eyeballs, deem the beloved donair to be "gross".

Or maybe it's just that they're not drunk enough to enjoy the full donair experience.

# There's Always Someone in the Kitchen at Parties

The 1981 hit by Jona Lewie often gets misquoted. The song is actually called "You'll Always Find Me in the Kitchen at Parties" and is about a loner guy who isn't very good at socializing, so he hides out in the kitchen where things are a bit more low-key. He chats up girls and eventually finds a mate, and by the end of the song declares that "he's done his time" in the kitchen at parties.

Over the years, our perception of the lyrics has been distorted. In an informal poll, only my music-geek husband, whose brain stores miscellaneous music-related trivia like a high-functioning computer (and who can correctly tell you the second song on side two of the Cure's third album – without looking – and can probably tell you where he was when he first heard it) was able to quote the correct lyric.

Everyone else I asked was certain that the song was called "There's Always Someone in the Kitchen at Parties."

We believe this revised lyric and title because there really is always someone in the kitchen at parties. It's funny because it's true, and because for most of us, some of the best parties we've been to in our lives took place not in rec rooms or fancy living rooms or rented event spaces, but gathered around a kitchen table.

The move to the kitchen tends to happen around the time teenagers start drinking. Up until then, parties are monitored, supervised or chaperoned by grown-ups, so toddlers all leaning against a counter with big red cups in hand, discussing politics or that hip new band, is an unlikely scenario. But once the opportunity to mix your own drinks arrives, the kitchen is no longer the place where mom makes the sandwiches and birthday cake, but rather a place where a kid can come into adulthood.

In the Maritimes, we've made a whole industry out of the kitchen party, but as I point out in the introduction, there's no real organization involved. People gravitate to the kitchen and the progression of the evening from that point forward is completely organic.

As a kid, my family never really had parties. Sure, "company" would come over, usually uninvited or spur-of-the-moment, and they'd end up in the kitchen, but I cannot recall an evening where my folks got dressed up and prepared an array of food and cocktails, with the purchase of the required bags of ice and the playing of music. And since I was at first a bit of a loser geek with no friends and then a funny-haired punk freak whose friends my parents wouldn't want in their house, I also never hosted parties as a teenager. I quickly made up for this deficit once I moved out on my own in 1987 at the tender age of 18.

You know what happens when you put two teenaged girls in an apartment of their own mere blocks from the downtown core? That's right, parties. Lots of parties.

My first apartment was a sub-let bachelor on the Dalhousie University campus in Halifax. It was a run-down hole, later demolished to make way for a science building, and at one point had no working lock on the door because repair guys from Dalhousie came and removed the whole door knob and never bothered to return and replace it.

I moved in with my friend Paul, but within a few weeks, we had decided that we wanted to move to Toronto when our sub-let was up at the end of the summer, and he moved back to his hometown of Antigonish where he was guaranteed a job and he could make some money for moving expenses. Having the small place to myself, I invited my friend Sharon to stay with me until the moving date arrived.

I'm not sure how the barbeque parties got started, but over that summer, it became an almost weekly tradition that most of the kids from Backstreet Amusements, a local pinball arcade frequented by Halifax's punk set, would show up at our door for one. The rule was that you brought your own food and booze, and every Saturday afternoon, twenty or thirty punks would cram into my two room bachelor apartment, cook lots of hot dogs, and get shitfaced drunk.

They spilled out onto the porch and spread across the steep and creaky old stairs, laughing, shouting, drinking and eating. Someone over 19 would make a run to the LC (the provincially-run liquor store) and fill orders for booze. Someone else would fire up my small hibachi and my roommate, Sharon, and I would sit back with glasses of lemon gin and tonic while pointy-haired kids rooted through our junk drawer for a spatula or tongs.

These parties caused a great deal of strife with our downstairs neighbour. An older woman, she lived in the basement apartment with her adult son. We were generally creeped out by both of them, particularly the son, who would let himself into the other apartments that had been vacated for the summer, and spend the day there by himself, hanging out. Given that the whole building comprised bachelor apartments, we guessed he spent his time on the vacationing tenants' beds. Eww.

Although the building was owned by the university, the downstairs neighbour was supposedly the landlady/caretaker, and she was constantly on our case about the noise. But she was afraid to come up and say anything directly, especially when there was a party going on, so she took to banging on the ceiling with a broom handle. Over the summer it became almost a joke and at the first bang, all the punks would rush into the kitchen and begin stomping like crazy on the floor in their huge boots.

The best part of these parties was the bring-your-own-food rule. Kids would show up with buns, burgers, hot dogs, chips, pop, booze, and even their own condiments. It got to the point that some were even bringing salads and casseroles. As the evening wore on and people started to leave, heading for the local punk nightclub, or the underage concert venue, or just back to the arcade, they'd realize what a pain it would be to drag half a bag of hamburger buns around with them for the rest of the evening and would leave their stuff behind. Sometimes they'd ask if they could come back the next day for their half-consumed bottle of vodka, but mostly they just left everything sitting on my cluttered kitchen table.

Working on the theory that anything left behind belonged to us, and that we were stuck cleaning up their mess and so were deserving of anything that was still good, Sharon and I would fill our fridge with their leftovers and consider it well earned. We ate an awful lot of hot dogs that summer, but it definitely cut back on our weekly grocery bill and left more spending money for Harvey Wallbangers at our favourite dance club, or a post nightclub donair on the walk home.

The kitchen of my first Toronto apartment, in Kensington Market, was tiny and smelled constantly of gas and dead cockroaches. It was maybe 10 feet long by 6 or 7 feet across. When Paul and I arrived in Toronto, it contained a run-down fridge and stove and a folding card table and two chairs, the table and chairs having been borrowed by one of our other roommates from an aunt in the suburbs. I remember that very first night in Toronto, being exhausted, hot, and bewildered, sitting on the sill of the open window to eat a bowl of curried glass noodles our roommate Gordon had cooked up.

While we did occasionally hang out in the living room to watch TV or a movie, this kitchen was where we spent most of our nights.

Our fourth roommate Derek was studying to be an interior designer and the kitchen quickly got spiffed up. We added some black and white tiles, a bookcase from IKEA to house dishes since the cupboards were tiny, and I contributed a beautiful rectangular white marble bistro table – with room for all of us to sit and eat at - purchased with a windfall back-pay cheque from the job I left in Halifax.

We'd sit at this table every night, drinking, smoking pot, eating ice cream, and doing all manner of stupid stuff that people get up to when they've also been drinking, smoking and ingesting too much sugar. We sang, we danced, we made stupid noises, we set traps for the never-ending parade of mice. We never thought to move the nightly party elsewhere; by then Derek had filled the living room with fancy furniture, bought on credit cards that were never paid off, and we were all too scared of spilling something on the white damask upholstery to feel comfortable there.

My next apartment had no official kitchen at all. Our original foursome had quickly gone sour; Gordon and Derek, who had been a couple, broke up, and Derek kicked me out of the flat to use my room as part of his expanded male escort service (which, in retrospect, explains how he could afford antique furniture and designer clothes). I moved three doors down to a place in a rooming house with another Halifax ex-pat.

Amanda and I lived in what was, literally, a garret – the sloped-ceiling attic space of an old Victorian row house, complete with a little balcony in the trees overlooking Kensington Avenue – where we shared a bathroom and a kitchen with some dubious characters. Food left in the kitchen would immediately be stolen by the other tenants, so we took to eating out or buying only what we could eat that day. And since the kitchen was never cleaned, we did little cooking there, mostly eating take-aways or piles of fresh fruit from the various stores in the market.

By the time I moved again, this time to a bachelor flat in a row house next door to my original Toronto landing place (for those keeping track, first at 38 Kensington, then 32, then finally to 36), Sharon had made the move from Halifax and had taken the basement apartment in the same old house, our flats connecting by an internal hallway and staircase. Derek had disappeared, and Paul moved back in with me, sharing two decent-sized rooms, one of which was a truly spacious kitchen that was the original of the hundred-year-old house. Again, many parties were had.

The most memorable of these parties took place in the winter of 1989. I started out the evening drinking cherry brandy and Coke. As people, mostly strangers, filled my apartment, I was getting progressively drunker. At some point, one of the ceramic tiles in the hallway to the back door had been broken, and every time someone stepped on it and knocked it out of place, I would yell, "Fix the tile!" indicating that they should, at least, put the broken bit back in place.

This sequence occurred so often that, as the evening progressed, everyone in the room began to join in on the refrain.

At some point in the evening, and things are a bit hazy here, a guest thought that I was a bit too high-strung with regards to my broken floor tile and suggested I get stoned. Specifically, he opened his hands to reveal about an ounce of magic mushrooms, telling me that I could have them all, for free, but I had to eat them all, right now!

Well, you don't have to ask me twice. I agreed to the deal and quickly consumed the 'shrooms, washing them down with even more cherry brandy. I don't remember much after that, really. I think we all had fun. But after a certain point, I was getting mighty tired of all these strangers in my kitchen, and since I have a tendency to become a weirdo clean freak when I'm stoned on hallucinogens ("Look at all that dirt. Can you see that? Oh my God, it's disgusting!"), I felt compelled to kick everyone out and mop the floor.

Except they wouldn't leave. So I did what any enterprising stoned punk girl would do, I enlisted muscle.

Bunch of Fucking Goofs were a local punk band and "gang" who, in the 1980s, were like Kensington's own security service. They "ran" the market and kept it safe, preventing a lot of crime from taking place. To the assembled party-goers, Steve Goof, the leader of the crew, was the unofficial mayor of the neighbourhood. So when my drug-addled brain decided that my kitchen party was done, I grabbed Steve, who was off in a corner, and said, "Steve, I ate an ounce of 'shrooms and these people are making my floor all dirty."

That was all it took for my hero to spring into action. Within minutes, Steve had cleared my apartment, hustling everyone down into the basement and into Sharon's apartment where the party was still going strong. He rooted through my broom closet and dug out a bucket and mop and proceeded to scrub my kitchen floor for me.

He even came back the next day and glued that stupid ceramic tile in place. Which wasn't too much extra effort on his part, considering that he had come by mainly to reattach the front door to Sharon's apartment, which had, at some point during the evening's festivities, been ripped from its hinges and was lying flat on her kitchen floor, covered in Doc Marten boot prints.

A few years later I had moved out of the market and into a warehouse space with my then boyfriend. Before the days of pretentious real estate agents calling them "lofts", units in old warehouses, predominantly used as studios, but more often than not, also as illegal residences, were simply know as warehouse spaces. Because they were a space... in a warehouse.

Our space in a back portion of an old factory building (where mattresses and then cheese had been produced), in what was then a very seedy part of Toronto's west end, was about as raw as they come, with exposed brick walls (and not the nice, pretty sandblasted kind), massive old heating pipes along one wall, and a concrete floor. We overlooked all of this because of two things: the unit came with a professionally installed loft level that looked down to the main floor at both ends, and a 40-foot cedar ceiling that made the long narrow room feel like a cathedral.

Because it was meant to be a work space, the only amenities it included were a small bathroom with a shower. We set to work building walls under the loft, creating bedrooms, and set up the kitchen at one end of the space, adding a fridge and stove, and building counter tops out of two-by-fours and some gorgeous reclaimed doors. The boyfriend attached rows of wire shelves to the wall and we filled them with old mason jars full of cooking ingredients. Technically it didn't have a sink, but the bathroom sink was an industrial washtub, making the place feel even more funky and artsy.

And yes, parties at this space still somehow ended up in the kitchen. Despite the huge loft area where we had set up our living room, it was common at parties to find it empty. Music blaring, strobe lights bouncing off the walls and the high windows, I would look down over the wrought iron railing into my tiny, galley-like kitchen to find most of the party guests there, leaning against the counters in conversation.

The best kitchen-party house I've ever lived in was an old Edwardian mansion in Toronto's Parkdale neighbourhood. Built in the early 1900s when the area was super-posh, the house was meant to be home to a probably large family and at least a couple of servants. There was even a twisting, steep and narrow servant's staircase running from the second floor to what would have been the original kitchen area.

The house was converted to flats some time in the 1950s, and by the time I moved in, it was somewhat worse for wear. The second floor apartment, where we lived, had probably been bedrooms and the massive kitchen, as best we could tell, was originally a storage area or passageway and a large summer porch that had been made into one room. Measuring something in the area of 15 by 15 feet, the room had a total of eight huge sash windows.

It was made into a kitchen without much forethought – the counter and sink in one corner, the fridge and huge old 1950s gas range in the other, making the classic cook's work triangle a bit of a hike, particularly when you were carrying a big pot of boiling pasta water.

In addition, the lone steam radiator was near the entrance to the room, while the wall of windows way across at the other side meant that it was almost unbearable to sit at the kitchen table on cold winter days, layer upon layer of frost forming on the inside of the thin, warped panes of glass.

Despite these obvious flaws, we adored this kitchen to the point of obsession, mostly because sitting at that kitchen table on a glorious summer day felt like being in a tree house.

Aside from the typical mature trees in most backyards in Toronto, we had a very special tree. Not more than 5 feet from the back wall of the house, someone at some point had planted a maple tree that had grown to five or six stories high. The base was so wide in circumference that two adults, hand to hand, could not wrap their arms around it. Planting this tree was, in actuality, a rather foolish thing to do, since by the time we lived there, the roots of the tree had destroyed the house's foundation and all sorts of issues with flooding and mold and shifting had started to occur.

But from inside my kitchen, what that tree meant was a gorgeous canopy of green each summer, sunlight dappling the table as I worked each afternoon, and a whole variety of birds that we courted with different types of feeders. In the dark of night, there was more than one occasion when I went into the kitchen for a drink and looked out the window to see a pair of shining raccoon eyes looking back at me curiously, the brave fellow having climbed up the massive trunk to enquire as to whether we might have a few snacks that we could spare.

And parties, oh parties at that old house were legendary. As always, the living room would be empty, although a dining room free of a table and chairs often encouraged dancing. But the real excitement was always in the kitchen, with friends crowded around the table or lined up along the counter. I'd move my butcher block off to a corner to make more room, and the servant's staircase was a quick escape route for the nicotine-addicted once I put a ban on smoking in the house.

Even in the summer when we tried to have parties on the back patio, that kitchen was like a magnet and eventually the mosquitos and the close proximity to the cold beverages drew everyone back inside where we could pretend we were in our secret tree house.

When my husband Greg and I started doing concert production and were bringing in acts from around the world, that kitchen hosted many a rock star for breakfast the day after the show. Big pots of coffee and baskets of muffins warm from the oven greeted them as they arose, and they were always so delighted to be treated with such hospitality.

During one weekend music festival, a dozen or so musicians and their gear filled my kitchen for days. They took over my stove to cook vegan food and slammed back tequila shooters at the huge wooden butcher's block. During that same weekend, we all sat transfixed around the kitchen table as a violinist from one of the bands sat below on the back deck and played for an hour, serenading the whole neighbourhood with his ethereal performance. Like the down east kitchen party, that weekend around the table, when we were not off at concerts, was like an organic thing that ebbed and flowed as people came and went, or as someone would clear off the empty bottles and chip bags and detritus to make room for a new round of drinks and snacks. While I'm proud of the great festival we all put together, my most vivid and cherished memories of that weekend all take place in my kitchen.

My current kitchen, I'm a bit sad to say, isn't really very good for parties. Probably because our current residence, an apartment that is a good size, but feels minuscule compared to that Edwardian ark where we lived before, isn't really great for parties either.

Don't get me wrong, it's a seriously cute kitchen, and the huge window that looks out over a garden and a row of pine trees was the deciding factor in our choice of this unit and this building (okay, central air conditioning might have swayed us a bit). But the layout makes it difficult for even two people to negotiate their way around efficiently, and the separate dining room means that the conviviality of being able to cook and talk to guests at the same time is gone.

No doubt, if I invited a pile of people over, they'd all find a way to cram into the kitchen anyway, but – and maybe I'm just getting old and crotchety here – I don't really think it would be all that much fun anymore.

Maybe, like Jona Lewie, I've done my time in the kitchen at parties.

# Part 2 – Toronto

Sheryl Kirby

# Kensington Market and the Flavours of the World

I arrived in Kensington Market on what might have been the hottest day of the summer. August 16, 1987, had been foggy and cool when my roommate Paul and I left Halifax in the early morning hours for our new home in Toronto. We wore black turtlenecks – I remember that clearly – and black leather jackets. Emerging from the crisply air-conditioned airport limousine, the heat and stench was like a punch to the face. I recall thinking, "What the hell have we done?" and grabbed my sewing machine that I had dragged with me as my carry-on luggage, and tried to climb back into the town car where I would convince the driver to take me back to the airport.

In the 35-degree-Celcius heat, what I was smelling was the late-summer miasma of a neighbourhood that claimed to have the largest selection of produce in one place, anywhere in the world. To a girl from Halifax, used to the air smelling occasionally of sewage from Halifax's utter lack of sewage treatment (for 250 years, dumping it in the harbour and letting it wash out to sea seemed like a spiffy idea), this smell was not only more offensive but also utterly unrecognizable.

Kensington smelled of anything and everything: rotting fruit, rotting fish, rotting tofu whey dumped unceremoniously in the gutter, fried bread, incense, non-rotting fruit that smelled rotten, frying garlic, a melange of Chinese spices wafting from the open back doors of restaurant kitchens in nearby Chinatown, chicken shit, natural gas (or rather the chemical they mix with gas so you know there's a leak), weird unidentifiable herbs, and pot. During my first few months living in Toronto, I was so paranoid about this smell permeating my clothes, hair and skin that I was known to ask friends and co-workers to lean in and tell me if I "smelled like the Market". Needless to say, it was complete and total culture shock.

Our first apartment in Kensington (there were a few) was a long narrow flat above a store. Our friends Derek and Gordon had moved in a couple of months previously, and when their third planned roommate fell through, they encouraged Paul and I to make the move and join them. I'm not much of a spur-of-the-moment kind of girl, but I had already concluded that my desired career path in fashion design wasn't going to get very far in Halifax, and I was easily lured by Derek's stories of the many vintage clothing shops that lined Kensington Avenue.

The flat was hot and dirty and stank like gas, but also something else, sweet and sickly. It was cloying and burned at the throat, and was often worse when the small stove in the flat's kitchen was first turned on. Months later, tripping on LSD, Paul would turn off the gas line and disassemble the stove under the pretense of cleaning it, only to discover that the gas pipes were actually packed solid with dead cockroaches. I stood by, also tripping on LSD and screaming in horror the whole time, as he used an old chopstick to push the thousands of dead bodies out of the pipe and into a garbage can. It was definitely more pleasant to cook things in that kitchen after that, though.

Vermin was an ongoing fact of life in Kensington. Besides the cockroaches, our decrepit hundred-year old row house had a multitude of mice. We caught 22 in one evening by filling and re-filling a trap with wedges of leftover muffin that I brought home from my job at a local coffee chain. One night there was even a rat. We had no idea where it came from, but we suspect a wrought iron heating grate in the living room. The four of us were sitting in the small kitchen, getting stoned on pot, like we did most nights, and we heard something running down the long tiled hallway.

By the time the creature had gotten down 40 feet of hallway to the back of the flat and burst into the kitchen, it had become bigger and scarier in our minds and sounded immense. We all four screamed as it came into the room, and what was, really, just an average-sized rat, made a screeching noise back at us and disappeared behind the stove. When we finally felt brave enough to get down from the stools on which we had been perched (and damn, don't I wish I had a photograph – three gay men and a fag hag, dressed to go out clubbing in the height of 1987 androgynous goth fashion, all standing or kneeling atop bar stools, screaming and flapping their hands helplessly), Paul had pulled out the stove to discover a hole that didn't seem big enough for a rat to fit through. But the thing was gone, and the guys boarded up the hole the next day, even though we weren't entirely sure it hadn't been a figment of our collectively stoned imaginations.

The other main form of animal life in the Market was chickens. While the retail sale of live birds had been banned a few years previous, there were still three separate slaughterhouses within a block of us; one Jewish, the second Chinese, and the last Portuguese, representing the three main cultural groups of the neighbourhood at the time.

Rows of trucks piled high with crates of live chickens pulled in and parked most nights of the week, starting soon after midnight. Coming home from the clubs, the market would stink of chicken shit, often to the point that one of us, usually not even that drunk, would throw up due to the smell. On colder nights when the smell wasn't too bad we'd still try to hurry past – those stacked crates of terrified chickens awaiting their death were just too sad to bear.

It was also common for some of the chickens to occasionally escape, and I'd find myself in the bathroom in the early morning, putting on make-up to head to work, and looking out to see half a dozen fluffy white birds making a break for it through the back alleyway, being chased by a frustrated white-coated Chinese man in rubber boots and a hairnet. The man would ultimately win out, though, and hours later, Chinese women in thick rubber aprons would walk down Kensington Avenue pushing dollies with open-topped plastic garbage bins strapped onto them, a creepy tangle of chicken feet bouncing up and down with every bump of the wheels, destined for the carts at the many dim sum restaurants that lined Spadina Avenue.

In terms of the non-living animal life, the many butcher shops and fishmongers in this small few blocks made for some interesting stories. Even though I had grown up with part of my family working in local grocery stores, and thus was familiar with being in the butchery department and dodging sides of beef hanging from hooks in the refrigerated work area, this would not prepare me to see men dragging similar sides of beef out of trucks and across Kensington's narrow streets, wet pools of blood forming on the asphalt behind them. One image that has remained with me for years is a chef from a local dim sum restaurant walking along the street with two dead baby pigs slung casually over one shoulder.

Likewise, growing up mere miles from some of Nova Scotia's fishing villages could not prepare me for the sight of a 300-pound tuna sitting on the sidewalk in front of a Kensington fish shop. Not to mention the baskets of live crabs, dying and stinking in the hot sun, that seemed to be everywhere we turned, especially in the summer.

At first, we didn't know much about the neighbourhood that we had landed in. There was no internet in 1987, so you had to actually talk to someone or use an encyclopedia to learn things back then. Our knowledge of Kensington Market came from the 1970s CBC series "King of Kensington" starring Al Waxman. A few years later, Sharon, another roommate who made the trek from Halifax, had the opportunity to meet Waxman's daughter at a party. When Waxman's daughter offered Sharon a ride home, Sharon was horrified to discover that the girl didn't actually know how to get to Kensington Market.

One of our favourite places in the area, probably because it was just foreign enough to be novel but not as scary and intimidating as the Chinese supermarkets with stuff we marvelled at but couldn't identify, was Switzer's. Switzer's was one of the last Jewish delis left on Spadina Avenue, from back in the day when Spadina was part of The Ward, a large neighbourhood of tenement slums that attracted first Irish and then Jewish immigrants.

At Switzer's, we revelled in our first experiences with smoked meat, really good bagels, egg creams, blintzes and my most beloved latkes. That the place looked cozy and familiar, like a retro diner, made us feel more welcome than the Chinatown restaurants where we didn't understand the menu. At Switzer's the waitresses wore beehive hairdos, pinned lacy napkins to their uniforms and called us all "Hon."

By the late 1980s, though, the Jewish community had mostly migrated north – Switzer's too would make the move a few years later. Spadina was all about the Chinese community, with a small bubble of Vietnamese, and Kensington, which had a Portuguese wave after the Jewish community moved out, was also filling up with Chinese shops and restaurants.

For a bunch of kids from the suburbs of Halifax, where "Chinatown" was one little shop, and Chinese food was chicken balls in Day-Glo orange Jell-o, we were both excited and tentative to try the different cuisines of our neighbourhood. The Dragon City Mall at the corner of Spadina and Dundas Street West was like being transported to another part of the world. Besides the shops selling everything from factory-made plastic crap to traditional kimonos and elegantly carved Chinese furniture, we spent most of our time in the basement food court. There, without the accusatory glances of the servers at the more formal Chinese restaurants, we ate our way around Asia. Mandarin, Szechuan, Hunan, Hong Kong, Vietnam, Laos... even Indonesia was represented, and I became a life-long fan of nasi goreng and gado gado. Fish sauce, hot sauce, peanut sauce; this was a world of flavours that ignited my palate.

We also couldn't keep ourselves out of the shops. We'd buy huge boxes of Chinese pastries, shrieking with a combination of disgust and delight at the grease that oozed out of a fried sesame ball and then eating it anyway. We bought slices of what we deemed "junk cake": a Swiss roll that seemed to be full of cream and bits and chunks of the other types of pastries; all of the stale "junk" that was left over from the day before. The Jamaican bakery in Kensington regularly served me breakfast – a warm fluffy coconut bun and a champagne cola (which was like a cross between cola and cream soda). While doing laundry, we'd raid the Portuguese bakery next door to the laundromat and buy piles of custard tarts and bacalau (fried cod fish balls) to eat while we watched our towels spin and bounce around in the windows of the dryers.

In Chinatown, once the vendors grew to recognize us and were amused at our curiosity, we tried jackfruit, lychee, mangosteen, and even the dreaded durian. In order to learn more about the food surrounding us, Gordon instituted 5-dollar Fridays, in which we'd each go out with 5 bucks and buy something to contribute to dinner. These meals didn't always work – there's not much you can really do with rice noodles, a hunk of jackfruit, fresh cream cheese and a chocolate cake – but it got all of us into the shops and talking to the people who worked there. What is this? How do I eat it? How do I cook it?

At the restaurants, my roommate Paul's biggest frustration was my inability to learn how to use chopsticks, and all of my roommates would groan with embarrassment when I'd ask for a fork. It got so bad that, at our favourite Vietnamese place, I'd purposely order the grilled pork chop because it came with a fork and knife. Paul tried to counter this problem by taking me to a shop that sold Sanrio gear and other items such as dishes, lunchboxes, and notepaper, all with cartoon characters on them, and buying me a pair of Snoopy chopsticks, made for little child-sized hands. I never really mastered them (I'm left-handed and often have trouble watching a right-handed person do something and then getting my brain to translate it), until the sushi trend hit a decade or so later at which point I became quite adept. I still have the Snoopy chopsticks and use them occasionally when I'm feeling nostalgic.

On occasions when we were particularly broke, Kensington proved itself to be the perfect place to eat on the cheap. Produce is always less expensive from the shops in Chinatown, and I'd start the day with a small mountain of fruit that usually cost me less than a dollar. When I was counting my pennies to put towards a silk velvet opera cloak at the vintage store where I worked (conveniently below my apartment), I'd make do at lunch with a trip to one of the cheese mongers, where they'd stuff a bagel full of slices of the cheese of my choice (Brie? Gouda? Stilton?) for a buck twenty-five. A dollar could also buy a Vietnamese bahn mi sandwich from one of the shops on Spadina, where they took a French roll and jammed it full of dubious meat or less dubious tofu, veggies such as shredded carrots, cabbage, and plenty of coriander with a liberal splash of hot sauce.

And it would be wrong to be 19 and not eat far too many packages of ramen noodles. At the Chinese supermarkets, there were entire aisles of hundreds of varieties and flavours of packaged noodles, most selling for 25 cents each. You just had to check the packaging carefully because the ones closer to the floor especially were prone to be chewed open by mice.

My second summer in Kensington, I cut my leg quite badly. Walking through the alleyway to the entrance of our flat, I stepped over a garbage bag that was full of unwrapped broken glass. A large piece, some 3 inches long by about 1 inch wide ended up in my calf muscle, hitting a major vein on its way in. As I stood at my doorway, gushing blood and screaming in pain, our neighbour Mei Ling came to my rescue.

Mei Ling and her family were originally from China. Her two young kids told us once that their father had been a dentist, but here in Canada, he did some kind of manual labour. Collectively, their English was poor, leading us to suspect that they were here illegally, and their living conditions (one room and a powder room – no bathtub or shower – at the back of a store) didn't exactly speak to their having family support. But when she came to my rescue, Mei Ling took it upon herself to take care of me when I returned from the hospital.

Despite my protests, Mei Ling sent one of her kids to our door at dinner time every night with a plate full of food for me. Although she couldn't afford to feed another mouth, she would accept no compensation, and when I tried to get her son to tell her it wasn't necessary, he came back with the message that because she had found me and helped me before the ambulance arrived, she believed it was her responsibility to take care of me.

So every night for two weeks, the plate would arrive. Always there was rice and a large chunk of tofu, with a rotating selection of vegetables and desserts. Most memorable were the sautéed boy choy and the cubes of black grass jelly, a dessert we had tried in the Asian food court and quite liked.

And while I didn't always enjoy these meals, particularly the tofu (the tofu factory two doors down that dumped its whey in the gutter out front had turned me off of everything soy until years later when I became a vegetarian), to Paul and I, these meals were a glimpse of Chinese cooking that we didn't experience at the nearby restaurants. Mei Ling's dinners were simple, but healthy, and showed us much more clearly how Chinese families were cooking and eating.

In the spring, Mei Ling showed us how to dry lychee fruit on our roof. We peeled the fruit and removed the large pit and spread them between two sheets on the flat roof above our entry way. The sheets kept the squirrels from raiding the stash, and the fruit were allowed to dry in the sun, to be preserved for future use. Mei Ling advised us not to eat too many lychee, lest we get "hot sick". She would say this repeatedly while touching her fist to her chest. Although Paul, who had trained as a chef back in Halifax, had been teaching her basic English in exchange for Chinese cooking lessons, we required her son again to explain what she meant. Too many lychee, especially dried ones, will apparently give you heart burn.

One last aspect of the Market that cannot be ignored was the garbage. I've remarked on how badly the neighbourhood could smell, and also that it was easy to eat cheaply there, but it should be noted that before it became a trend – hipster, environmental or otherwise – people foraging through garbage for free food happened in the Market every single day.

Since so many of the shops sell produce, there's always a high amount of loss or waste: an apple with a bruise on one side, greens that have wilted and cannot be revived. Every night the fruit stores would put their garbage out at the curb, with the "this could still be good" category of items on top. By 6:30 or 7pm, when the shop owners had disappeared, leaving the market to the rats and punks and the potheads, the garbage pickers would arrive to do their grocery shopping, coming with their own baskets and working their way through the wooden crates, being careful to leave things tidy as they moved on to the next shop.

It's been more than two decades since I've lived or worked in Kensington. I seldom even shop there anymore. But when I walk through the streets that seem not to have changed at all, I feel more at home than anywhere else in the world. It may be because despite the push of chain store and condos, the Market has remained steadfast. This is a world of family-owned shops and small indie restaurants. This is a neighbourhood that welcomes wave after wave of immigrants and asks nothing more from them than to share their culture, especially their food culture. Alfajores and tacos rub elbows with pho shops and dim sum and Middle Eastern baklava. Jewish halva can be had across the street from German bratwurst, which is just around the corner from the vegan cafe and the French bistro known for serving horse meat. Local ice cream, local craft beer, pies made with local berries – all exist in harmony with Indian spices and curious imported fruit.

It may be a form of urban myth when people say that Toronto is the most multi-cultural city in the world. But when I wander through Kensington Market and Chinatown, I believe it to be true. At least when it comes to the sights, sounds, flavours. and smells of the food. Had I arrived in Toronto back in 1987 and lived in any other part of town, I definitely would not have the love of food and cooking that I do today. Kensington wasn't just home; it is part of who I am.

# The Gaffe

From the outside, it looked so much like a bomb shelter that we didn't go near it for the first few weeks. Dropping a bunch of kids from Nova Scotia into the middle of Kensington Market and Chinatown was pretty much akin to setting us loose in a candy store. We spent those last few weeks of the summer of 1987 exploring the neighbourhood and completely disregarded the gem directly in front of us.

By the time our Maritime crew descended upon Toronto, Cafe La Gaffe (better known as "The Gaffe"), was a Kensington Market mainstay. One of the few restaurants in the Market at the time, the little unpretentious French bistro represented a level of cool that we weren't quite up to yet, despite our aspirations of glamour and delusions of grandeur.

From our second floor apartment directly across the street, The

Gaffe was all boho chic; the old Victorian building was fronted by a series of porches and add-ons and corrugated roofs of different colours and materials from metal to a clear blue plastic.

The two patio tables in the front spilled onto the sidewalk. If people were seated at them, anyone walking past would have to step into the gutter to get by. But from this spot, customers could nurse a coffee or a glass of wine and sit on a Saturday afternoon and watch the world go by. Coming from Halifax, where patio tables only existed in the backyards of the well-to-do (most people had picnic tables), this seemed to us to be the ultimate in urban sophistication.

When we finally got up the nerve to venture across the street to eat there, we were welcomed warmly, already recognized as Market locals. Inside was just as funky as the outside with Middle Eastern shawls serving as tablecloths and wine served in juice glasses. The floor was a mishmash of concrete and creaky wood, the walls uneven plaster with a mixture of artwork – some local, some posters of famous works. It felt as if it had not changed in fifty years and we imagined ourselves as retro beatniks. Heck, I already had the beret.

You could still smoke in restaurants at that time, and I remember the air being a blue haze, especially thick when you consider the long room was essentially open to the street. I can't for the life of me remember ever going to the washroom there, although I must have at some point. I should come clean and point out that many of the hours I spent at La Gaffe were in some sort of drunken haze.

Kensington at night took on an otherworldly quality and felt almost like a movie set. The old Victorian buildings loomed over the street while people picked through the cartons of refuse in front of the various produce shops, looking for discarded fruit and vegetables. From the two front patio tables, you could look up into the double windows of our living room, and it felt eerie to sit there after dark and watch my roommates move about, dancing and laughing.

The smells of the Market and nearby Chinatown perfumed the front of The Gaffe as we sat and sipped beer and watched the Market empty. The rich kids from Forest Hill who had come downtown to buy used jeans disappeared before dinner time. The shopkeepers were gone by 7pm, after they'd hauled their discards to the curb. A few genuine diners remained, but the place emptied early and the front tables were always ours as only the creatures of the night (the punks, freaks, artists, and potheads) stuck around.

It was at the Gaffe, over glasses of red wine, plates of bruschetta and many, many cigarettes that we fought, discussed, reminisced, and planned for the future. Young, beautiful, and with our whole lives ahead of us, we felt invincible on those nights, fuelled by wine and unfiltered Gitanes. My roommate Gordon fancied himself a superhero one night and created a persona; Kevin 7-11 righted wrongs, defeated injustices and helped little old ladies across the street.

A year later, allegiances broken, I no longer lived across the street from The Gaffe with a pile of beautiful and adoring gay men, but one door over (they say you can't ever really leave the Market once you've lived there), and I worked not in the vintage shop below my apartment but in one across the street. The bistro remained our after-work hang-out – bottles of beer and bowls of Asian rice snacks fuelling jovial conversation between the local vintage vendors as we recapped a day of wacky customers or fabulous finds. Sitting there in the late afternoon sun, I no longer felt invincible, but I remained happy nonetheless. I knew that joy, that place, those people, wouldn't be there forever, but at Cafe La Gaffe, time always seemed to stand still, and for the duration it took me to nurse a beer or two, I could pretend that things would always be that good.

Cafe La Gaffe was gutted by a fire in the early 1990s. Shortly after, it re-opened on Baldwin Street near McCaul Street, part of a strip of restaurants that mostly cater to office and hospital staff from nearby University Avenue. While the owners tried to maintain the atmosphere of boho chic that made the original location so special, the very different clientele and the distance from Kensington Market proper meant that La Gaffe's days as a Market hangout had ended.

Other French bistros have since set up shop in Kensington Market, but none ever possessed the allure and the magic of Cafe La Gaffe.

Sheryl Kirby

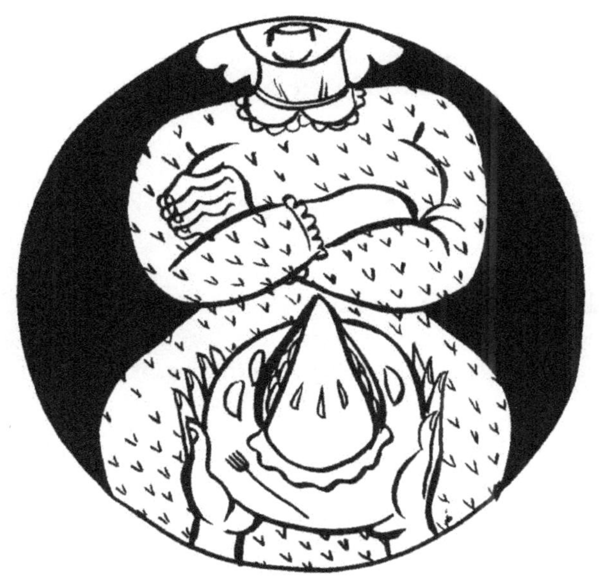

# Pie For Breakfast

I baked an apple pie yesterday. We had a curiously overwhelming number of apples in the house that needed to be used up. Presumably, I bought them all, but for the life of me, I cannot explain how or why I acquired so very many of them.

I generally prefer tart apples for pie-making but my selection was varied: a few bright Granny Smiths that sat in the bowl on the table glowing neon green in the sun; a couple of Spartans; some small organic Galas that showed up in the weekly organic grocery box; and a few large Fujis, mottled stripes of red and yellow skin beckoning me to eat them out of hand and not sacrifice them to the heat of the oven.

Displaying uncharacteristic patience, I managed a halfway decent piecrust, the one baking task that is always hit or miss with me. I seemed to make better piecrust as a child, or maybe I'm just airbrushing my memories and am substituting my mother's exceptional crust for my own. In any case, it came out pretty close to perfect, and the pie itself is delicious. I even remembered to pull it out five minutes before it was finished so I could apply a light brushing of milk and sugar to the top.

This morning, I ate a piece of my apple pie for breakfast. I ate it cold from the fridge, with a few small slices of cheese. The crust was light and flaky, sparkling sweetly with sugar, and the apples were soft and infused with cinnamon and nutmeg. Each bite was topped with a small sliver of smoky cheese and the dogs sat before me drooling intently, hoping for all their lives that I'd save them a small wedge of the crust at the end.

Many years ago, I would travel to southern Ontario with my then-boyfriend for holiday weekends. These trips involved making it to Brantford by bus or by train to his mother's house, and then his grandfather would come and pick us all up and drive us back to the family home in Simcoe. As long as the ex and I were together, this was the standard practice for Thanksgiving, Christmas, Easter, and usually the civic holiday in August.

One Thanksgiving, upon arriving at the house in Simcoe, my ex's mother began making an apple pie for dessert with dinner on the big day. I sat in the kitchen to keep her company, watching her hands move deftly as she manipulated the dough and quickly peeled the apples. As she was assembling the pie my ex popped his head into the kitchen and stated, "Sheryl puts nutmeg in her apple pies!"

By the reaction this comment garnered, you'd have thought he said "Sheryl tortures puppies and force feeds them to little children!"

Nutmeg! Can you imagine? Sacrilegious! My ex's mother looked at me with steely clarity, the intent of her words clear but laced with hidden meaning that I'd only come to recognize years later when the ex and I split up; "There will be NO nutmeg in THIS pie!"

Okay, no nutmeg it is, then.

On the day after Thanksgiving, the ex and I got up and began rooting around in search of breakfast. His mother and grandparents had already eaten a hearty breakfast of homemade oatmeal, and the ex and I were not enticed by this option. Instead, we figured we would eat the last two slices of the apple pie.

"You can't eat PIE for breakfast!" came the resounding decree from both grandparents and mother.

"Why not?"

"Because, it's pie. Pie is not breakfast food."

"It's fruit and pastry. What's the difference between a slice of pie and a danish? Or a muffin? It's certainly healthier than a poptart," I replied, gesturing at the decades-old box the ex's grandmother had unearthed from the cupboard.

"No, no, no… it's pie. It's a dessert item. You can't eat it for breakfast."

"Sure we can. We're not going to fall over from malnutrition by eating one piece of pie at an unusual time of day."

To ongoing protests, we sat down, each of us with a cup of tea and a slice of apple pie in front of us, and proceeded to devour the flaky pastry and sweet fruit. Through the thick haze of cigarette smoke that followed the ex's mother everywhere she went, we watched her as she shook her head in disgust and disappointment. What a terrible influence I was on her adorable perfect son.

For our part, we savoured every bite, letting the flaky bits of crust melt on our tongues as the syrupy sweetness of the apples exploded in our mouths. It was a sweet victory for us, disapproving adults looking on and clucking their tongues. The only thing that would have made the scene entirely perfect was if the flavour of the pie had been a little more pronounced. A little bit of nutmeg would have been ideal.

# The Fruitcake Missionary

Every year there's at least one of them. The fruitcake-hater. They're a timid lot. Someone, at some point in time, has put "the fear" in them. In many cases, it was years ago; some manufactured atrocity handed out at the office, or Great-Aunt Bertha's dry stale creation that's been handed back and forth from branch to branch of the family for a dozen years or more.

I take my work as a fruitcake missionary very seriously. The thrill of the challenge must have been what brought the religious zealots back to the south seas islands again and again for the chance to convert the heathen natives. Fruitcake really is better than no fruitcake, you just have to trust me. Have faith, my friends, and follow me to the light.

The first step is to treat the fruitcake-hater with a sense of gentleness. Move slowly, so as not to startle them, make no quick movements towards the buffet table. Just enquire, with a sense of caring and concern, as to exactly why they feel so vehemently against an innocent dessert.

The usual response is sullen. "I just don't like it."

Yet when you press further (cautiously, mind you), it's easy to uncover that, in most cases, they haven't eaten a piece of the much-hated cake since childhood. Some will have specific complaints: they hate the nuts, they hate the fruit. These few are lost causes, and are better left to graze the cheese plate. As long as the ingredient of annoyance is included, they'll be difficult to convince.

The others, however, the ones that complain of dry, hard cake with brittle marzipan icing, these are the ones that are ripe for the picking. "Oh, but see, I never use marzipan. Unless you make it yourself, it tends to taste chemically, and it does dry out. Plus it makes it really difficult to soak the cake with booze."

Now you've got them. Their eyes light up brighter than the lights on the nearby Christmas tree. "Booze, you say? What kind of booze? Great-Aunt Bertha was a tee-totaller. She never used booze."

"Well, I make two kinds of fruitcake," I explain, "a regular one with orange brandy, and this nifty tropical version with pineapple and papaya, plus cashews and macadamia nuts, all soaked in more than a cup of coconut rum."

At this point, most fruitcake-haters will emit a low, hushed, "Oooooohhhhh."

"Would you like to try some?"

Most will hesitate initially, put off by memories of the 3-to-4-pound cakes that typify the season, figuring they'll be expected to eat the whole thing, or at least a large slice.

"I make them in a couple of sizes, see? I make regular cupcake-sized ones for the people that really love fruitcake, and then I make these little mini ones for people who just want a taste. They're the same size as those little two-bite brownies. It's a two-bite fruitcake. Surely you can stand two little bites? Here, try one of the tropical ones."

This is when the fruitcake missionary gets to stand back, smile smugly, and chortle quietly to themselves. The fruitcake-hater's eyes invariably become round and happy at the first bite. "Hey, this is goooood!" they exclaim. "It's not like that dry hard fruitcake at all. It's like the batter is really just a transport vehicle for the booze-soaked fruit!"

From there, many will even move on to the regular fruitcake of their own accord. By the end of the evening, most are fully converted and are trying to figure out how to get themselves on the fruitcake gift list for next year.

I am the official fruitcake baker for my family and my husband Greg's. While Greg's grandmother still bakes fruitcake for friends and neighbours in her hometown, she prefers to eat mine. No small compliment from someone who ran a hotel kitchen for 40 years and has been baking for most of her life.

Unlike those south seas missionaries, I don't ask my converts to be devout. They don't need to pray or give alms or put on pants and cover themselves from the Lord's sight. All they have to do is be a little bit open-minded and try it. Just once, just one bite. All I have to do after that is sit back and wait for them to sing in praise.

Sheryl Kirby

# Show Me Your Mussels

I had been craving lobster for weeks. Ever since I had some in Halifax early last month, I wanted more. Lobster, being an expensive treat regardless of where you live (even at home, in the middle of lobster season, four decent-sized ones cost us 50 dollars), is something that I might eat once every three or four years, usually on trips home. My last feed might even have been in 2000 during a trip to PEI, in the beginning stages of my conversion to vegetarianism (which never made it past the stage where I ate fish), when my mother-in-law offered me lobster sandwiches because everyone else was eating meat pie. But once you get the bug for the buggy creatures, you can't stop the craving. Lobster is sort of like the crack of the sea.

All the signs yesterday pointed to a lobster dinner. There were omens, you see. As I was walking the dogs in the morning, we passed a torn bag of garbage: lobster shells scattered across the sidewalk by some raccoons looking for a late-night delicacy. In the newspaper, a ditzy writer's entire column was about eating sushi and watching a chef prepare lobster sashimi, in which the lobster's tail is ripped off while it is still alive.

While I wasn't exactly that brave – I stick to the pot of boiling water and repeated apologies method – I was determined to have lobster for dinner. I would go crazy if I didn't have that tasty crustacean dripping juice and melted butter on a spread of newspapers. It should be noted that this really is the only way to eat lobster, the butter actually being optional. While there are plenty of creative, and supposedly tasty, ways of preparing lobster – arranging the little fellow in a decorative manner so he appears to be waving, for instance – they're really not very practical. It's difficult to eat lobster in polite company without ending up covered in juice and butter, and those bibs they jauntily tie around your neck give an otherwise classy event the look of a two-year-old's birthday party.

So I sent Greg off to St. Lawrence Market with a list. The mistake was in sending him to a beer-tasting event first. By the time he reached the market, our preferred fish-monger had one sad little lobster left in the tank. Instead of checking the other places, he came home with 3 pounds of mussels.

Now, I like mussels just fine. They're not as good as clams, but they're tasty and I seldom have complaints when a plate of mussels is placed in front of me. Except when I'm expecting lobster. I even had the big pot out and ready to go. What the hell was I going to do with mussels?

Lobsters, you see, are a meal unto themselves. Somewhere fancy, you might get side dishes, but at home, you just eat lobster. Mussels needed stuff to go with them. Foresight had compelled my husband to nab a loaf of crusty French farmer's bread. Good, excellent, but not enough. Frites really are the necessary thing with mussels, especially if they're in a basic sauce. But at 34-degrees-Celcius yesterday, it was far too hot to make fries in my un-air-conditioned kitchen. While Greg went out to nab some french fries from the falafel joint at the top of the street, I got to work with the shellfish.

There are many restaurants that offer "mussel menus", where you can have mussels and your choice of thirty or more sauces, from curry to pesto to Ethiopian Berebere. At home, though, unless you live by the seaside and can cook them in a giant pit full of hot rocks and seawater on the beach, the best and easiest is a simple sauce made with lots of onion and garlic sauteed in olive oil, liberally doused with salt and pepper. Once you add the mussels to the pot, a bottle of blonde lager (a nice spicy one is best) is all you need.

Between the plates of frites, the loaf of bread, the glasses of beer to drink, and the extra plate to catch the shells, we covered most of the table. With a fan placed strategically to simulate an ocean breeze and save us from the heat, we dug in. It quickly became apparent that mussels were the perfect choice for the evening. Lobster is always tasty, but it can be so rich that in hot, hot weather, the flavour is almost nauseating. Mussels, however, in a light beer-based broth, were exactly the right thing: filling, but not gut-busting. We pulled the fleshy orange meat from the shells and dipped it back into the beer. The frites also got sloshed in the beer broth and the slightly sweet crusty bread was perfect for scooping up all the onion and garlic floating in the bottom of the bowl.

With the bread and fries, 3 pounds between us was slightly too much, the standard pound per person would have sufficed. The extra pound allowed us to have seconds, however, a decadence not accorded by any means when you order mussels in a restaurant. There was even a few handed out to well-behaved puppies, who determined mussels to be very tasty indeed, and who offered up cute tricks and paw shakes in an effort to entice just a few more out of our bowls and into their drooling mouths.

So I had hoped for lobster, but at a quarter of the price, mussels turned out to have been a far better choice, both from a financial standpoint and a personal satisfaction one. There's a metaphor for life in that analogy somewhere, but now I'm too hungry to analyze it further.

# Two Grapefruit

I am craving grapefruit: cold, wet, sweet, a blast of juice, and so many vitamins I can feel them pulsing through my veins, working hard to fight off the cold virus currently wracking my body with chills and a hacking cough. I want nothing so badly as I want the tangy burst of citrus on my dry and pasty tongue.

When I was a child, grapefruit was something that was placed before me in my favourite bowl, ready to eat, carefully halved and sectioned with a grapefruit knife by my devoted grandmother. All traces of membrane had been studiously removed, sugar had been lightly sprinkled across the exposed pink flesh, and a cherry sat provocatively in the centre to cover the hole where the stem once resided. Like a small princess I would eat each section, carefully, cautiously, tasting for tartness, and demanding more sugar where necessary. If I was feeling especially prissy, I'd call on my overworked grandmother to come and scrape down the sides for me, to retrieve the last bits of pink sweetness still clinging to the thick skin, lest I angle my spoon the wrong way and send a spray of juice across my face and into my eye.

Now a grown-up lady, living far away from my grandmother, I have no choice but to prepare my grapefruit myself. This is probably why I eat the things so seldom. Grapefruit are a lot of work, and within my extensive collection of kitchen utensils, the curved serrated blade of a grapefruit knife does not reside.

Yet I have grapefruit. In the green beaded fruit bowl that shimmers with movement as the cat bounds across the table, two grapefruit sit waiting in the sun, amongst the more often preferred apples, pears, and bananas.

I want grapefruit so badly that I am sure one will not be enough. I pick up each, weighing them in my hand, checking the skin. They are soft from sitting here for so long, a week or more. I take a knife and cut a wide X in the top of each, placing them both in a bowl and returning to the table with a large cloth napkin. The dog appears by my side, interested in anything that might pass as food.

"You don't like grapefruit… do you?" I ask suspiciously. He'll eat almost anything, this one, but a few hated items such as mushrooms are always spat out onto the floor with an audible "Pleah!" I cannot remember if grapefruit is one of these reviled foods, and I am hesitant to have my precious treasure end up on the floor.

I plunge my thumb in to the cut of the first yellow-skinned globe and begin to peel. This one bears a brand-name sticker, abandoned in the bottom of the bowl, indicating that I've purchased it at the supermarket. Pieces of thick skin fall into the bowl below. As I carefully peel back thin sections of the bitter pith, the almost neon pink flesh is enticingly revealed. The skin removed, the edible part of the fruit appears frightfully small. I plunge both thumbs in now and pull apart the sections into quarters.

The pink cells are sweet, slightly dry, and just a little tart. My hands covered in juice, I pull away at the section membrane so the wet pulp is exposed. Wonderful.

A wet nudge at my elbow reminds me that I'm expected to share. Through skeptical eyes I watch as the whiskered face beside me carefully accepts the proffered section of fruit. Gently, he takes the wondrous treat, being ever so careful not to nip my fingers with his sharp teeth. Yes, delicious, more! He appears to like grapefruit after all.

I make my way through the sections, bit by bit, peeling away at the tough fibrous membranes and exposing the soft sweet pulp. I am regularly reminded that it's nice to share, and then suddenly, it's gone, devoured by the dog and me.

I attack the second fruit with much gusto. I was right – one was not enough. This grapefruit is an organic one, packed into my weekly box and delivered to my doorstep. As I peel away, the skin on this one noticeably thicker than the other; I feel disappointment; the grapefruit has let me down. The flesh is white. Oh, how terrible, the white ones are always sour and bitter. Briefly, I consider tossing it in the composter; it will be awful, it will ruin my delight at the fruit I've already eaten. I eye the dog beside me – will he eat it?

Here goes nothing, I think, as I break the grapefruit into quarters, juice squirting up into the air. Expecting that my face will pucker and turn inside out at the bitterness, I am delighted, astounded even, at the sweetness exploding in my mouth as I take the first bite. This grapefruit puts the other to shame. There is no comparison whatsoever. I cannot believe I even considered the other one to have any semblance of flavour. This is heavenly, with each bite of the pale, sweet pulp, I feel my health restored.

I look down at my companion who is staring at me expectantly, a long thin strand of drool hanging from the side of his mouth and almost – almost – touching the floor. "This one is too good to share with dogs!" I declare, attempting to put him off, but his willpower is stronger than mine and I give in. "Fine," I sigh, rolling my eyes and giving up a piece to his slobbery mouth. Together we finish the thing off, relishing each sweet section, each small cell of pulp, until suddenly, as quickly as its inferior predecessor, it's gone.

I am not believed when I make this announcement, and it is only after I submit the bowl for inspection and a good sniffing at the bitter pith and peel that the grapefruit is deemed to be officially finished. The dog, having done his part to assist, wanders off, leaving me to dispose of the skin, wash the bowl, and wipe the wet squirts of misdirected juice from the table, wishing that I had at least a dozen more.

# The Nabe

My glasses steam up as I walk inside. It's a warm day and this small café with the open kitchen is noticeably hot. The take-out coffee counter is busy and I strain to see if an empty table is available. It's the wobbly purple one by the entrance to the kitchen, but it's got a good view. Before I even sit down, there is coffee before me and my order has been taken.

It's an odd place this, a corner location that was probably, at one point, a small grocery store. It's surrounded by houses, and there are no other businesses for blocks, which makes it seem a bit like a cozy oasis. It's been here for years, as much a part of the neighbourhood as the church on the next block or the school across the way.

I am not the only lone diner this morning; in fact, there are a few. We sit with steaming mugs of coffee and reading material before us:

newspapers, novels, magazines, even some paperwork and a calculator. Near the window, a young family takes over the biggest table, spilled juice and a stuffed rabbit jostling for room amid the plates of pancakes and the omelette of the day.

Who are all these people who have the leisure of sitting in a neighbourhood café on a balmy weekday morning as if they have no other care in the world? What delightful twist of fate has allowed us all this small luxury? There's the family, all laughing toddlers and uncombed hair. Two separate older gentlemen, each reading the paper. An elderly couple. A pretty slim brunette in front of me, her nose deep in a book. And a couple of young stay-at-home moms with their toddlers in tow, all impeccably dressed given the fact that this is probably their big outing of the day.

My food arrives; the hearty oatmeal pancake taking up most of the plate, the saucy roasted potatoes scrunched over to dip their edges in the creme anglaise, and the slices of fresh fruit hanging precariously near the rim. This is what I came for, but the ambience is fulfilling too.

Out in front, I can see through the wide plate glass window that a few locals have gathered with kids and a dog to have coffee in the warm November morning. At the picnic table covered by a wide green awning, they laugh and joke as soft brown sparrows flit from the nearby apple tree, looking for crumbs. Inside, the well-dressed toddlers are remarkably behaved; they do not screech or cry, they sit politely and sip carefully at too-full glasses of juice and nibble at muffins as their mothers chat animatedly in their hip skirts and silk hairbands and trendy eyeglasses.

The overhead fan is turned on and the air cools slightly. On the walls, paintings of naked women are framed in old windows, which makes you feel slightly voyeuristic, as if you've caught a glimpse of someone stepping out of the bath.

A toddler from the family table at the front comes towards me and waves. I admire her pink leather slippers and remark how I'd like a pair of my own; her mother, hot on her tail, smiles and agrees with me. Beside us, another little girl shows off her silver ballet slippers. I am envious of the shoes of a three-year-old.

It is good, this place – welcoming and warm. None of us know one another, yet in this moment, we are a family. We smile at one another, we all stop to pat the dog at the picnic table on the way out. We all walk away full of warmth and goodness, and the happiness of a leisurely morning breakfast at a neighbourhood café, even those of us who sat alone.

Sheryl Kirby

# Cravings and Squicks

*Warning: Discussion of vomiting ahead.*

Food (being, ideally, a sensual pleasure) is one of those things that we either really love or really abhor. Individual foods, I mean.

As children, we go through phases where we dislike different things – based on taste, texture or smell. As we age, those tastes usually adapt and progress, and we willingly eat spinach or beans or whatever food it is we hated so ardently in our youth.

The one exception to this rule is when food becomes associated with a traumatic event, particularly something physically traumatic like a serious illness. Watching it all come back up can turn us off from ever desiring a particular food again.

When I was a kid, my mom was a big fan of cream of tomato soup.

She always added additional milk to our soup, in part to cool it and additionally to make it creamier. Except one day, the soup was too hot and the milk curdled, although I didn't know it until the first spoonful. I haven't been able to eat cream of tomato soup since then. I can't, to be completely honest, even watch other people eat it, especially if they break crackers into it.

Crackers and jam was the first solid food I was offered once after a bout of stomach flu (which conveniently began while racing around Halifax Harbour in a speedboat – we all thought I was just seasick at first). I can eat crackers with anything else on them, I will happily and joyfully eat jam on anything else, but thirty years later, I cannot eat crackers and jam together.

Cannot is the wrong word to use, though, because obviously I am capable of eating a simple cracker with jam on it. It won't kill me, and I think I've even done it under duress at least once. But the idea of crackers and jam sets something off in my head that sends me hurtling back to my little pink bedroom; I can picture the bed linen, the curtains, the toys and books, the collection of Barbie dolls, and that plate of crackers and glistening red strawberry jam than went flying onto the floor as I made a dash for the bathroom after the first bite.

A recent bout of stomach flu has done pretty much the same thing. Almost all the foods I ate the day it hit are now verboten. I can't, suddenly, stand the smell of my beloved home-roasted coffee. The thought of the bread pudding I had at a local café for brunch that day freaks me out, and the dear, unassuming piece of lemon meringue pie I ate when my stomach first started rumbling and I simply assumed I had coffee gut and needed more food, may well be lost to me forever. Is there life without coffee and lemon meringue pie? I may have to discover.

More intriguing than the squicks is what I find myself craving. Once I had consumed litres of Gatorade, apple juice, and flat gingerale, and the idea of solid food came back minus the shuddering, it was actually to my childhood I went again. Chicken noodle soup, damn the vegetarianism, would be the only cure. Then vegetable soup with beef broth. Both had restorative powers, despite my ethics. A tub of raspberry sorbet wedged into the back of the freezer officially became my favourite food ever. I even found myself craving Granny Smith apples – thin slices, exactly like the ones that garnished my plate of bread pudding. Theoretically, the apple should be off the list, but perhaps because it was crisp and fresh, it's allowed to stay as a "good" food.

My brain seems to have a category it refers to as "clean, fresh food" that it leans to in times of physical crisis. Hangovers, the day after acid trips back in the 1980s, and recovery from illness all demand salad. Not swank fancy salad with sun-dried tomatoes and olives and cheese, just iceberg lettuce, tomatoes, cucumbers, and maybe some grated carrot.

And French dressing. No, I don't know why. I didn't even have French dressing in the house today for my salad binge – I had to dig out a recipe and make some, but French it had to be, all brilliantly reddish orange and tangy. This was not the time for single-origin olive oil and fig balsamic vinegar and freshly chopped herbs. My homemade stuff wasn't quite as satisfying as if it had been the cloyingly sweet bottled stuff (or better yet, if the entire salad had come from Red Lobster, complete with croutons and a slice of cold Bermuda onion), but I do have to draw the ethical line somewhere, even when it comes to cravings.

Over the next few days as my body recovers and I start eating larger portions of richer food again, all of these cravings and squicks will fade away. Of course, I will go back to drinking coffee, absolutely I will patch up my spat with eggs and cheese, and citrus fruit (I threw up a whole glass of orange juice) will go back into regular rotation. But in the meantime, I am curious to learn what my body (and brain) thinks it wants and doesn't want.

I tried to convince myself that I could continue to eat like this forever – little tiny portions of light but nutrient-packed foods – but I know it won't happen. Eventually I will answer the call of chocolate and red wine, or a nice hunk of aged Mimolette. Definitely the devil's starchy fingers in the form of double-cooked French fries. Or perhaps Red Lobster or something significantly worse.

The body wants what it wants and right now, it's my job to see that the good stuff goes in and the bad stuff stays out. I am but a servant to a precocious and temperamental master. But eventually, my equilibrium (and my hedonistic diet) will be restored.

*Postscript: This piece was written in 2007 after a bout of Norwalk Virus. I am still, regrettably, unable to eat lemon meringue pie without freaking out.*

# Prosciuttotarian

I've fallen off the wagon. I blame my husband Greg. He fell first and dragged me down with him.

When I started food writing, I did make a resolution that I would "sample" things when I had the chance, just for the sake of expanding my palate and increasing my knowledge about food. I've been doing that when the opportunity arose, but with little enthusiasm; the prosciutto and salami I had at a recent event didn't wow me, the burger Greg ate last week grossed me out (I spit out the tiny bite I tried), and the massive brontosaurus-sized ribs he ate for lunch on Saturday made me think that I had maybe just lost the taste for meat. I got them down and it wasn't gross, but it wasn't a pleasant taste – just kind of… dank. Maybe that's why ribs need so much sauce – to cover up the yucky grey taste.

Then we wandered into St. Lawrence Market and a nice man handed me free prosciutto.

I always had this running joke that I'd like to be a prosciuttotarian. Pescetarians are folks who eat fish, but are otherwise vegetarian. Pollo-vegetarians eat chicken. I wanted to be able to eat prosciutto. And somehow I always knew that prosciutto would be my downfall.

I tried to convince myself that the piece I had a couple of weeks ago was typical, and that I just found the stuff far too salty now. But then I had good prosciutto, and it was what I remembered it to be, and it was the one thing that I can honestly say I missed (other than the roast chicken I've wanted for the past few months, a craving that might also have to be rectified while I'm down and out and mercilessly having animals killed for my own hedonistic pleasure).

Something overcame me; I dragged Greg back to the stand and we bought the prosciutto. I felt guilty about it almost immediately. I felt guilty bringing it home; I felt guilty today as I made sandwiches on ciabatta buns with buffalo mozzarella, sundried tomatoes and pesto; I felt guilty while I ate the thing. But I did eat it. And moaned with more guilt about it later.

Karma works in strange and humorous ways, though. Because it was only about an hour or so after I ate the sandwich made from a poor little pig – when my sinuses got all congested and my throat swelled up slightly and I remembered – I'm allergic to pork.

All of my other allergies have mostly disappeared in the past year since we moved from an old house that we believe was full of black mold. Cheese is my friend again, even the blue stinky stuff, and ice cream and I are tentatively getting cozy. I assumed the pork allergy was gone too. Not so much.

So that was my first and last dip into the pool of meat-eaters, at least in terms of eating a large amount of meat at once. Small samples don't seem to set me off, but a whole serving certainly does.

In a way, it's good. I think that every vegetarian should go off the wagon at least once to really appreciate where they are. I learned that I don't really miss meat all that much, and that I don't really like it that much anymore. I enjoyed the lovely ham sandwich as far as taste goes – it was definitely delicious – but I can likely go another seven years or more before I need prosciutto again, and between the guilt and the not breathing thing, it really wasn't a worthwhile trade-off.

I might still need that roast chicken before I swear off the land animals completely, however. I can only hope I've developed an allergy to that too.

# We All Know Where the Rainbow Goes

*We all know where the rainbow goes,*

*We're told it's a pot of gold.*

I'm eating chocolates and it's bittersweet. I had been craving "box o' chocolates" (as opposed to the swank organic, fair-trade, single-origin stuff I usually eat) and grabbed a box of Pot of Gold the other day. They're getting hard to find.

The Pot of Gold brand was developed in the 1920s by a confectionery company in Halifax, Nova Scotia called Moir's. Moir's had started in 1815 as a bakery, but by 1873 it was exclusively making candy and chocolates. Moir's was actually the first company to come up with a mixed assortment box, and the Pot of Gold was an instant hit, becoming and remaining the best-selling boxed chocolate in Canada for decades. In most of the Maritimes, it wasn't Christmas without at least one box under the tree, although you might find rival Ganong as well. And unwrapping a box of Pot of Gold undoubtedly provoked a sing-a-long, as voices rough from too many eggnogs the night before sang the lyrics from the television ads, with almost nobody able to hit the high note on "gold".

Moir's was sold to Nabisco brands in 1967, and in 1975, moved across the harbour from its location on Argyle Street in Halifax to a modernized plant in Dartmouth. Hershey acquired the Nabisco confectionery division in 1987 and expanded the Pot of Gold line to a variety of assortments.

In recent years, poor old Pot of Gold hasn't been doing so well and the plant in Dartmouth is slated to close by December of this year. Besides putting hundreds of workers out of a job, it destroys the last vestiges of a company that got its start almost two hundred years ago and that has been a part of Halifax culture for just about everyone in that city.

I can remember the old factory on Argyle Street only vaguely. My mother worked nearby and the couple of times I visited her at work as a child, I remember the smell of chocolate permeating every part of the downtown. I also remember when the factory was being torn down (I would have been seven) to make way for the Halifax Metro Centre, and thinking how sad it was that the wonderful smell of chocolate would be gone.

So interwoven are these chocolates with my childhood memories that I based a novel around the old Moir's factory and the Pot of Gold chocolates. It hasn't been published yet, but now, more than ever, I am determined to do so, to help keep a piece of Halifax history alive.

I've seen different statements on the fate of Pot of Gold. Hershey originally announced its intention to sell off the Pot of Gold brand because "it does not fit our corporate strategy." (In other words, it wasn't selling well.) There's a lot more variety out there now, so people have more choices. Hershey's also messed around with the collection too much, making Pot of Gold dark, milk chocolate, and caramel collections, and removing a number of old favourites from the original. It's not Pot of Gold without my roman nougat!

The latest indication seems to be that the collection will remain but the jobs will move to Mexico, where pesky things like unions don't get in the way of profits. Moir's never had a great reputation for the treatment of its workers back in the early days, but unionization improved that situation. Nova Scotians bought the chocolates regardless because they were locally made (and back in the early days, were probably all that was available), and because doing so became a long-standing tradition.

This will be the last Christmas when a Nova Scotian-made box of Pot of Gold will pass under the Christmas trees of Canadians. Even if they are still available, coming from Mexican factories, it just won't be the same.

Time to stock up before the rainbow fades.

*After this piece was written in September 2007, production of Pot of Gold was moved to Mexico and the original collection was over-hauled with many of the long-standing favourites removed. Emphasis now appears to be on the more exclusive collections such as caramels and nuts and the chocolates seem to be available only around the holidays.*

## Dream On

One of the really fabulous things about summer is that it keeps me out of the supermarket. Buying all my fruit and veg, cheese, eggs, honey, and the small amount of meat we cook at home from local farmers is time not spent trolling the aisles being tempted by junk food. In the winter, though, when most of the markets close, my weekly excursion to the local grocery store is fraught with peril. I do my best to stick to the perimeter, although needing flour or dried beans or toilet paper always calls for a trip down the aisles, but sometimes those supermarket folks get sneaky and move the processed food over by the real stuff.

Which is how Greg and I happened upon a giant display of boxes of Kraft Dream Whip. We approached the row of boxes with caution.

Arranged behind a selection of wizened, tired-looking California strawberries, we understood that it was meant to be an impulse purchase – the temptation of berries and cream (an allusion to, if not an actual taste of, summer) in the midst of a barren winter's deep freeze.

Greg tentatively plucked at a box, flipping it over to read the instructions. "How do you make real whipped cream?" he asked.

"You, uh... whip some cream. With a bit of sugar and maybe some vanilla."

"Huh. To make this stuff you need to add milk and vanilla," he replied.

"Then what's the point? Why not just buy cream if you have to buy milk anyway?"

Greg read over the ingredients. "Mmmm… hydrogenated vegetable oil," he said. "This is full of trans fat."

He put the box back and we wandered through the store, griping about the crap that people will eat to save a few bucks. But if you've got to add milk and vanilla anyway, it can't be that much of a savings over buying cream, so what is the allure of foods like Dream Whip? You still have to whip the stuff – it's not a time saver in any way. It's not a convenience food that can be made just by adding water. So what makes it so popular?

I came home and poked around on Google. First I looked for ingredients, which the Kraft website conveniently does not include, probably because it's not information it wants people to read – or understand.

This is what Wikipedia says is in powdered whipped topping mix:

> *sugar, dextrose, partially hydrogenated vegetable oil (coconut and palm kernel oils), modified cornstarch, propylene glycol monostearate (emulsifier), sodium caseinate (from milk), and less than 2% of cellulose gel, cellulose gum, hydroxypropyl methylcellulose, natural and artificial flavor, acetylate mono- and*

*diglycerides (emulsifiers), sodium silicoaluminate (anticaking agent), yellow 5, yellow 6.*

Nice. Know what's in real whipped cream? Cream. Plus sugar and maybe vanilla, to taste.

Then I did a search on nutritional info. And then I understood Dream Whip's appeal, despite the crap it's made from. It's the calories, stupid.

A 5.2-ounce serving of Dream Whip (equal to 147grams, and incidentally, 10 tablespoons!) has 10 calories and 0grams of fat, even though it's made from transfats. A roughly equivalent serving of whipped cream (equal to 150grams) will run 520 calories and 55grams of fat.

But does anyone need 10 tablespoons of any kind of whipped topping on their dessert?

Dream Whip lets people buy into our sense of greed while feeding us junk and chemicals. It lets people cut back without making real long-term changes in how they eat, while pretending they're doing something positive like cutting calories.

If you don't want the calories that come with real whipped cream, then eat less. Have 5 tablespoons instead of 10, or even just 2. Eat the real stuff less frequently and appreciate it more. Or don't add whipped topping to your desserts at all. Eat it plain, or use a nice, naturally made yogurt, which is just as good.

Is this really a route people are willing to take to cut calories? And even if you do eat the crap and lose weight, aren't the health risks from eating so much fake food higher than the risk of being fat?

# You Should Just Buy

I was at the corner store, buying baklava to have with tea, when I discovered myself in line at the cash in between two separate men buying multiple bags of injera; the flat, spongy Ethiopian bread. Served with every meal, injera is used in place of cutlery to eat the variety of wats (stewed dishes) that comprise the typical meal.

Because I am my father's daughter and have picked up the habit of chatting to strangers, I joked to the guy behind me, "Is this as good as homemade?"

Apparently Ethiopian folks who have immigrated to Canada don't make their own injera. The mitad, the flat pan the bread is cooked on, doesn't fit on our modern stovetops. In faltering English he also said, "It's also hard… to get right… when it is prepared…"

"When it's fermenting?" I asked, and his face lit up. "I've always wanted to try and make it," I said. "My husband and I eat Ethiopian food a lot."

He shook his head. "Even our ladies have hard time. You should just buy."

Now I want to try it more than ever. But the teff, the grain used in injera, is expensive, so I'm worried about screwing it up. Maybe I should just keep buying my injera at the Hasty Market. If it's good enough for the local Ethiopians, who am I to argue?

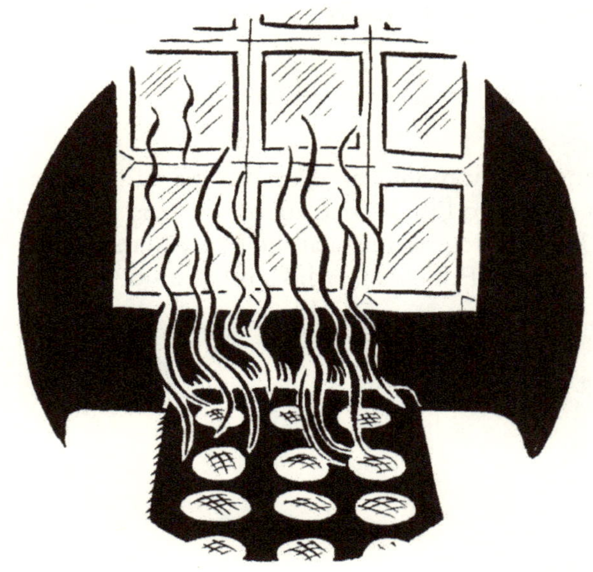

# In Defence of the Peanut Butter Cookie

A strange thing happened to me in 1991. All of a sudden my peanut butter cookies started coming out hard – like rocks.

I have no idea where the recipe came from. It was the one my mom always used, so it likely came from my grandmother, a cookbook, or perhaps a home economics course when she was a teenager. It is exactly like the majority of recipes for peanut butter cookies found on the internet today, where creators of "original" recipes try to differentiate themselves by incorporating an extra quarter cup of peanut butter or by sticking a chocolate kiss on top.

In all likelihood, however, every peanut butter recipe in use can be traced back to a recipe that first appeared some time in the 1930s, but most likely in 1936.

Which never explained why my cookies had started turning out hard.

At first, I blamed myself. I must have screwed it up somehow. But subsequent batches were also hard. I adjusted quantities and techniques, even considered that the oven might be acting up. Then I thought to consider the peanut butter itself.

In the early '90s, the western world was going through a bit of a phase of environmental activism. I took these concerns to heart and started to change my purchasing habits, switching to all-natural or organic ingredients where I could find them. I was also, at the time, dating a guy whose relatives lived next door to a peanut farm so all-natural peanut butter because a fixture in our house.

It was then that I realized what had happened. In switching to a freshly ground, all-natural peanut butter, I had drastically altered the recipe without even knowing. The all-natural brands tout the inclusion of nothing but peanuts, while the grocery store brands are loaded with fun stuff such as corn syrup, shortening and icing sugar to keep it from separating.

In fact, commercial peanut butter was created in 1922 when J.L. Rosefield of Rosefield Packing Company of Alameda, California, created a process that kept the oil in peanut butter from separating. This "churned" peanut butter included other added ingredients that made the product smoother and creamier and also kept the peanut butter shelf stable.

So, since 1922, most peanut butter available commercially has been "processed" in this manner. Which means that the original peanut butter cookie recipe was undoubtedly made with processed peanut butter, not the happy, healthy, natural stuff. And without the added corn syrup, shortening, and icing sugar, no version of the recipe works.

Figuring that out is, by all means, a eureka moment. But it's also a disappointing one; for anyone who wants to avoid the added crap, not to mention transfats (shortening is hydrogenated), regular peanut butter is off the list. And so are peanut butter cookies.

Given that peanut butter cookies are one of those comfort foods that bring back sweet childhood memories of working in the kitchen with my mom, I get cravings for them now and then. I usually head to a store or bakery and buy a couple, and that seems to satisfy the need for the things. But for home cooks, part of the experience of comfort food is in the making, and just eating ones that someone else has made isn't enough. I need to roll the dough in my hands and then oh-so-carefully press those distinctive crosshatch marks on the top with a fork. This was my job in the process as a little girl, and it brings back definite feelings of happiness and delight.

After Hurricane Katrina in 2005, I started keeping a pantry stocked with canned goods. Just to be on the safe side. Toronto had also experienced the Blackout of 2003, so having some stuff on hand just in case couldn't hurt. For some reason, while buying stuff to stock that pantry, I grabbed a jar of regular peanut butter. I'm not sure why. Maybe under the theory that it would keep longer than the natural stuff. But I came across it a week or so ago, and have had peanut butter cookies on the brain ever since. I finally caved and made a batch last night, for the first time in probably 15 years or more.

I know they're full of corn syrup and transfatty shortening and extra sugar. I don't care. They're that perfect combination of sweet and salty, with a crunchy bite on the outside that gives way to a soft tender interior. I know I lose all of my organic-local-sustainable food cred, but it doesn't matter. Sometimes food is emotional and emotions transcend nutrition.

# Crazy Pineapple Lady

Last night, Greg and I went for dinner at a local Indian dosa place in the far reaches of our 'hood. I used to go to this restaurant about once a month or so when my friend Melissa lived nearby. She was home during the day, as was I, so I'd walk up to her place and we'd go for dosa then do some shopping at the nearby mall. When she moved away, I had little reason to be in that part of the neighbourhood, and hadn't been back to this restaurant in a couple of years.

One of the things I always ordered was a pineapple uppatham. Similar to a dosa in that it was like a huge airy crepe, this was made by mixing chunks of pineapple into the batter before it was cooked. But it seems that I was the only one who ever ordered it and the owner took it off the menu during the time we were regulars. There were plenty of other great things to order, so it wasn't a huge deal, but it's always been my favourite.

Last night when we were there, the owner came over to take our order and recognized me. "You used to order the pineapple uppatham," she said. "I have pineapple today, do you want me to make one for you?"

I was delighted, of course – not just that I was getting my favourite dish that was no longer on the menu, but that she had even remembered me. I relished every bite, dipping the pancake and chunks of pineapple through the spicy coconut chutney that accompanied the uppatham.

As we finished, the owner came to take away our trays. "I have pineapple pudding today, would you like some?" Sure, why not, we figured, even though we were incredibly full. She brought us a dish of stewed pineapple, cooked down in a sugar syrup, spiced with cardamom, and coloured bright orange like fried jalebi pastry. It was fabulous.

"You want some more to take home?" she asked, as we cleaned the bowl. She explained that the stewed pineapple was a dish that she had made especially for her family and staff – it wasn't on the regular menu. This was why she had the leftover pineapple with which to make my uppatham, and she even said that she had thought of me earlier in the day when she had been making the dessert.

At this point, we were getting a little freaked out – both by the odd coincidence of me walking into her restaurant on the very day she had been thinking of me and had leftover pineapple, but also by the possibility that maybe she thought of me as some kind of crazy pineapple lady. We ended up bringing home two servings of the stewed pineapple dessert. I'm about to have it with yogurt for breakfast.

After this, though, a moratorium on pineapple for a while. You see, I actually bought a huge pineapple last week at the grocery store, so we have been eating it almost every day for the past week – it's been in smoothies, grilled and served atop rice pudding, and thrown into stir-fries. Crazy pineapple lady has had quite enough pineapple for a while.

# Quincy

Toronto is known as "the city within a park". Just about every resident lives within walking distance of a park, although most of these are not huge multi-acre swaths of land, but rather are little in-fill parkettes. Parkettes pop up in the middle of residential streets, and at one point, probably had houses on them. Now they are mostly home to swing sets, jungle gyms, and a few benches.

The parkette closest to us, the place where we end up a couple of times a day while walking the dogs, has some landscaping along one side. It's hard to tell if the city planted the bushes and shrubs or if they predate the park back to when there was a house on the property.

Last year, I joined a group of locals in cleaning up the park, as it regularly attracts crack dealers and hookers from the area.

Underneath the hedges and shrubs, we came across a pair of quince bushes. The bushes were covered in vibrant scarlet flowers in spring, and piles of little green orbs in the summer.

Regular quinces grow on trees and get as big as apples. Quinces are, in fact, part of the same family that includes both apples and roses. But these were tiny fruit, about the size of crab apples. I had wondered if the fruit were edible, and a neighbour who is involved with the local horticultural society couldn't tell me, but my Google-Fu told me that what we had stumbled across was an ornamental quince from Japan, appropriately known as a Japonica quince. Further Googling determined that Japonica quince were not only edible, but also made awesome jam and jelly, because of the natural pectin.

So one evening last week, once the temperature had dropped below freezing – which is when quinces are ready to harvest – I headed to the park and picked about 6 pounds of fruit. I hacked up my hands and wrists in the process – quince bushes have thorns – but I had a huge bowl of fruit to work with. The smell in my kitchen was just astounding, a cross between super-ripe tart apples and wild roses.

Oddly, I had no qualms about "stealing" the fruit from city property. Maybe I've been watching too many of the "local and seasonal" British TV shows, where town councils are allowing guerrilla gardeners to grow produce in sidewalk planters for anyone who wants it, but it's not like anyone else was going to make use of these quinces. And even the squirrels won't touch them because they're so bitter, so why not collect a few and make something fabulous with them? They'll just sit there and rot otherwise.

Prepping Japonica quinces for jam or jelly is pretty easy. You just chop them up and toss them in a pot, covering the fruit with water and letting the whole mess boil. Everything gets strained through some cheesecloth, so it's not necessary to worry about seeds. I cored most of the fruit anyway, afraid that the seeds might make the jam bitter.

Quinces have seeds about the size of apple seeds, but about ten times as many. Cutting into a fruit was like running into battle – a dozen or more seeds would go flying across the room, making a tiny rat-a-tat-tat, like machine gun fire as they hit the wall. Out of 6 pounds of fruit, I removed probably 1 pound of seeds.

From there, it's all about boiling. Recipes I found online suggested a cook time of 6 - 12 hours (!), but my miniature quinces cooked to a pulp in about 15 minutes. From there I sieved the pulp to strain out the seeds and skin, ran it through some cheesecloth and ended up with about 6 cups of super-tart quince pulp. Quinces are so tart that they're truly unpleasant to eat raw, and the acid in the fruit ended up burning away at my fingers where I had been coring the fruit with my thumbs.

After consulting a variety of recipes, none of which was especially helpful since they all appeared to have been written in medieval times, or required contraptions to hang the pulp overnight to let it strain, I went with a 1-to-1 ratio of quince pulp to sugar. Into the pot, let it boil to the "skin" stage (when a spoonful is dropped onto a plate, it quickly forms a skin), and then into the jars it goes. I added a little bit of cardamom as well. And that was it.

Not to toot my own horn, but hot damn, my quince jam rocks. For comparison, I grabbed a jar of Lebanese marmalada (a more traditional quince jam) that I had in the fridge. The flavour is just sugary and jammy, the colour a dark brownish red. The jam from the little Japonica quinces is an orangy yellow colour (the same as the fruit when fresh); is sweet, but bright and puckery at the same time; and has notes of pears, and tart apples, as well as floral notes of rose.

I put most of my jam into larger containers to keep and eat, but I also did eight small jars to give away at Christmas. I don't know if I'm going to be able to part with the stuff, though, or if there will be any left in a month. But I know that next summer, I'll be taking better care of the shrubbery in the park so that come October and the first frost, I'll be jamming it up with an even greater quantity of Japonica quince jam.

# Buffalo Gals

First, an admission. I am not as well travelled as I'd like to be. While I've been to most major cities in the US and Canada, I've never been across the big pond. Given my feelings about the environmental impact of travelling for pleasure, not to mention the fact that I just hate the process of travelling in general (waiting in airports, getting felt up by security, being jammed onto a plane for hours next to someone with toxic perfume, etc.), it is unlikely that I will end up seeing a lot of the world in my lifetime. Living in Toronto, that's not really a big issue, as I'm lucky enough to be able to hop on a cross-town streetcar and be transported to Athens or Seoul or Bombay for the very reasonable cost of 3 dollars, but there are occasional things that even the wonders of globalization cannot bring to the most multicultural city in the world.

Things such as buffalo mozzarella, which are consumed near where they're made and generally are past their prime by the time they reach a destination on another continent. I always figured that until I was able to travel to Italy, I'd never get to enjoy the real stuff.

Oh, I'd eaten bocconcini, made locally from pasteurized cow's milk and sold in tubs. Slightly softer than regular mozzarella, I found the stuff to be pretty bland and tasteless, although the various sizes of little cheese balls were fun to put in salad. I never really got the "silky" description though – most of what I ended up with had the consistency and bounce of one of those hard little superballs you could get in gum machines as a kid. You'd whip them at the floor and they'd bounce forever off of every surface, until your mom would come and yell at you to stop, lest the thing take out a piece of the Royal Doulton collection. Suffice it to say that in the grand realm of cheese, bocconcini really wasn't near the top of my list.

Then Greg called me from the aisles of fine food shop Pusateri's. Did I want some real buffalo mozzarella? I was recovering from the stomach flu at the time but said sure, as long as I didn't have to eat it right away.

When I finally got around to opening the cheese – it came in a sealed plastic tub – I wasn't expecting much. We had some nice ciabatta buns, some decent local tomatoes and some fresh basil to make sandwiches. I peeled off the wrapper and drained off the whey, holding the single tennis-ball sized lump of cheese in my hand. Right away, I could tell the difference.

The consistency was soft, squishy almost, and when I sliced into the cheese, it cut unevenly. Silky is a great description of this cheese because the texture was almost exactly like silken tofu. I split the ball between the two sandwiches and drizzled both with a mixture of a rare fruity olive oil and some fig balsamic vinegar laced with fleur de sel.

Flavour-wise, there is no comparison with the pasteurized cow's milk version. Even after its long journey and time spent in my fridge, the buffalo milk cheese had a sweet tang and smelled of grass. What I mean to say is that it actually HAD flavour, whereas the stuff we have access to most of the time tastes like nothing, just bland and white. To the tooth, the buffalo mozzarella gave way, crumbling almost and falling out of the edges of the sandwich. The rubbery bounce we were accustomed to was not there at all.

At 10 dollars for 200 grams, this is obviously going to be more expensive than your supermarket bocconcini, but it's comparable to many other good imported cheeses (for instance, aged Mimolette runs about 14 dollars for the same quantity). It's a high-fat cheese; 100 grams has 23 grams of fat, close to half of the recommended daily intake (the sneaky little Canadian nutritional label shows a serving size as being 28 grams – about one-eighth of the ball – HA! with only 6 grams of fat), so even without it being hard to find, it's definitely not something you could eat every day.

All things considered, the lack of availability is probably a good thing. But if it shows up again, we will definitely treat ourselves. After all, a trip to Pusateri's is cheaper and easier than a flight to Italy.

# Tomato Envy

There are bushel boxes of Ontario Roma tomatoes at my local supermarket. For some totally crazy inexpensive price like $14.99. Stacks and stacks of them, huge boxes the size of bales of straw. Bored grocery stock boys could make the best fort out of this display.

I slow as I walk past it. I circle it, once, twice. I could come back with the big shopping buggy, I tell myself. A bushel (53 pounds) would fit in the big cart.

I could make sauce. Oh, yes, sauce. And dry some, for the winter.

Wandering off to the canned vegetables aisle, I price the cans of tomatoes that I usually use for the soups, stews, pasta sauces and pots of chili I make with regularity throughout the year. My own sauce would be so much cheaper. And fresher. And tastier.

Who am I kidding?

It's not to be. There just isn't enough space. Okay, I'm not willing to make enough space. Certainly, corners could be found to stash jars of tomato sauce. Under the sofa, at the backs of already stuffed closets. We could scatter them around the apartment like little Easter eggs, coming across them with a squeal of delight during a cleaning spree or when lying prone in front of the furniture while retrieving a ball the dogs had lost control of.

But there is no official room for jars of tomato sauce. I've used up all the pantry shelf space making jam. My inclination would be to freeze the stuff anyway, but I've got five chickens coming from my friend Jeff's dad's farm, and last year they got to 10 pounds each before he slaughtered them. And my freezer, while still a free-standing chest freezer, is wee. Not to mention that I haven't even poached and frozen pears yet. No room in the freezer for tomato sauce.

And no room for the empty jars in the off-season.

I know some people do it. They find space because it's important to them. It should be important to me too, I think. But the thought of rearranging our storage closet, of pulling out old boxes of photo albums and Christmas wrapping and plant pots to find a place for tomato sauce… maybe next year. We'll clean the closet, purge some stuff we don't need, and clear a foot or two of shelf space for lovely, luscious sauce made from bright local Roma tomatoes.

But this year, all I can do is dream and watch with envy as the little Portuguese and Italian ladies, who don't look as if they weigh the equivalent of a bushel themselves, carry off cartons of tomatoes to make sauce.

Sheryl Kirby

# How to Make a Lobster Roll When There's More Than One Maritimer in the Room

We were lucky enough last week to be in on a delivery of Nova Scotia lobster. It seems that, once again, the supermarket chains are undercutting the fishers and are offering a dollar less per pound than it would cost to catch the things. So one enterprising guy from Yarmouth decided to fill a truck with lobster and head to Toronto. Word went out through a local CSA network and at the appointed date and time, we all showed up, happy to pay 7 dollars a pound – a couple of bucks less than the cheapest local price and 3 dollars more per pound than the chains were offering the fishers. There were even some local restaurants getting in on the deal, and the general consensus was that it was the best lobster we'd ever had outside of the Maritimes.

Greg and I were relatively conservative, buying only a half-dozen. Our plan was to eat a couple, put two more into risotto and freeze the meat from the last two to pair with fiddleheads in a quiche at a later date. That didn't happen, of course, because last Saturday, despite having had lobster for dinner the night before, we both had a hankering for lobster rolls.

The lobster roll is a speciality of the Atlantic provinces. McDonald's even offers them in Nova Scotia. They do show up in the occasional fancy restaurant, but they are, for the most part, a roadside treat, purchased while driving around places like Peggy's Cove; sweet chunks of fresh lobster meat presented on a soft white bun.

Problem is, there are as many ways to prepare this simple dish as there are Maritimers. And none of us can agree on the correct way to do it.

As I pulled the meat from the lobsters, Greg was dispatched to the store for buns and side dishes. Potato salad is a typical accompaniment, but he opted for that neon green coleslaw. Acceptable. Potato chips – fine. He brought me back a thick-crusted white bun, possibly of Portuguese or French origin – the kind of thing I'd expect a Vietnamese bahn mi to be made with. The ideal bun for a lobster roll is soft, like a hotdog bun. Most of the ones I've ever had down home are served in the squarish hot dog buns with the slit cut in the top as opposed to the side. No matter, we're making the cosmopolitan version, okay?

Then I made the mistake of asking Greg, "How do you like your lobster meat prepared?"

As I mentioned, no one can seem to agree on what goes with the lobster in a lobster roll. Some people make theirs with just the lobster meat and the bun, maybe some salt and pepper. I've also seen the same combination with a drizzle of butter. More complicated (and we're getting into potentially sacrilegious territory here) is a slather of mayonnaise on the bun before the lobster is added, and the full monty is to take the lobster meat and toss it with a dollop of mayo.

"Well," Greg says, "I usually have it salad style, with some chopped onion and celery."

I make a goggled-eyes faced and manage a "Whaaaatttt?"

"Celery and onion? Usually?? What is this 'usually'?" I demand to know. "We've been together for sixteen years. I've never made lobster rolls. How can you have a 'usual'?"

"Well, it's how my mom and grandma make it."

Ah. mom and grandma. Celery and onion. Shutthefrontdoor. I will compromise and mix the lobster up with some mayo, although I am more of a slather on the bread kind of girl myself. But there is no way I am putting celery and onion on that lobster. No fucking way.

As I'm plating stuff we decide that lobster rolls really do need a soda to go with – we still have to strive for some level of authenticity, even if we're not getting ocean breezes and the screech of seagulls overhead. So Greg went back out to the store for a bottle of Pepsi, because despite our ideas of the perfect lobster roll being so divergent that we might eventually have to divorce, we can both agree that only Pepsi will do for this classic Maritime treat.

# This Is Why People Go Out for Brunch

I cook breakfast. Every day.

Some days I do nothing more than put some fruit on cereal, but most mornings, Greg and I eat a real breakfast: buckwheat pancakes; quinoa and maple-glazed trout; scrambled eggs or sometimes oatmeal.

So when the weekend comes around, I am more than happy to toss aside my spatula and go out to brunch.

Despite the sheer hatred restaurant cooks and servers have for the weekend morning meal, brunch has been proclaimed the new dinner and Toronto's love of brunch has endured for decades. Brunch is comparatively cheap compared to a multi course dinner. It's relaxing and informal. And most importantly, people like to go out for brunch because it allows them to eat foods they wouldn't, or couldn't, cook at home.

Many breakfast dishes are fussy, with multiple ingredients, all cooked á la minute, and if keeping two pots and two frying pans and maybe the oven all under control at the same time isn't your cup of tea, going out for brunch, where someone else can do the juggling for you, probably is.

My plan this morning was to make crepes. I had a container of leftover sautéed mushrooms in the fridge from the mushroom pastries I made for dinner one night last week. I also had a bag of spinach that needed to be eaten. Spinach and mushroom crepes seemed like the answer, but the thought of singeing my fingertips while manually flipping the crepes had no appeal.

I pulled out a couple of multi grain bagels and figured I could do an Eggs Florentine kind of thing, only without the eggs. Bagels and spinach and a mushroom cream sauce. Then Greg walked in and I stupidly asked him if he wanted it with eggs.

"Eggs are good," he says. And then I think about whether I'm up for wilting spinach, building a sauce, toasting bagels and poaching eggs all at the same time.

"I'll do the eggs," he says. "I can do them in the microwave."

(A word of warning to you all; if your spouse ever offers to poach eggs in the microwave, immediately insist that they take you out for brunch.)

Happy to have one less task, I agree, and Greg goes about finding instructions on the intarwebs for microwaving poached eggs, then dumps eggs into bowls with water and vinegar and pierces the yolks so they don't explode.

All goes relatively well until the eggs start coming out. Even though he followed the instructions, microwaves are finicky things and the egg yolks are totally hard. We plate them anyway, as everything else – bagels, sauce and spinach – are all hot and ready. I poke one of the eggs yolks with a knife to see just how hard-cooked it is and…

KABLOOOOEY! Egg-explody.

Every surface within a 2-foot radius is covered with egg. And then my darling husband says, "Good thing that didn't explode inside the microwave, huh?"

Because apparently, cleaning the egg from inside a small enclosed box is more of an effort than wiping egg off the wall, the counter, the toaster, the food processor, the sides of the cupboard, underneath the cupboards, the floor, my face, my shirt, and yes, down my cleavage.

The most frustrating part is that had the eggs been poached properly, with lovely oozing yolks, the dish would have been an absolute wonder (despite the mushroom sauce being kind of grey). With half-exploded overcooked yolks, it was still good, but not amazing.

Next time, I'll do more of my prep ahead of time – finish the sauce and keep it warm, wilt the spinach and then reheat it in the microwave if necessary, all so I can pay attention to properly poaching the eggs.

Or I can insist that we go out for brunch and someone else can poach the damn eggs instead.

Sheryl Kirby

# You Like Shop Chinatown

It's that invisible, emotional umbilical cord that ties us to our past. Chinatown, especially when it's hot, reminds me of that day in August 1987, when I stepped out of an airport limousine and into a different world.

The stench hit me even before the heat that day, and as long as I lived there, I wondered if I carried the smell with me, if I invaded nightclubs and restaurants perfumed with the odour of durian fruit and greasy bread and sesame oil and fish.

Today, my quick tour through Kensington Market and Chinatown is mission-based. Beads of sweat forming on the back of my neck, I want to get what I need and get out.

I don't dally in the market, hitting the health food store and the fruit stands for what I need. It's too hot, and I want to be home in front of a fan. On Spadina Avenue, in the crush of bodies and racks of knock-off Hello Kitty purses and cheap luggage, I move with purpose, sliding gracefully around the tourists and the delivery people pushing dollies full of boxes. Like riding a bike, this way of moving through the crowd, looking up to assess the sidewalk, shifting as necessary, comes back easily. This is my 'hood. Get out of my way.

After a quick stop to grab a Vietnamese sub and cold chow mein noodles for my lunch, I brace myself for the Chinese supermarket. Down the stairs, past the sidewalk displays of produce and dried shrimp, the smell is damp, salty, with a vague undertone of rot, and reminds me of the caves and grottos along the Bay of Fundy when the tides have rushed out, all wet sand and Irish moss.

Produce. Nothing is labelled in English, and I guess at herbs, packed in cellophane, feeling lost because I cannot make my way through foreign territory by smell. Thai basil I know by sight. The strong smell of cilantro permeates the plastic. I have no idea whether I'm buying peppermint or spearmint, but into the basket it goes.

Next, fat wet Japanese udon noodles, and a package of oil-fried tofu. Then down the aisle to the intimidating wall of noodles. Thirty different kinds of rice paper wrappers for spring rolls – different sizes, flavours and brands. Vermicelli noodles, enough to tie a string, if placed end to end, around the world. Ah, sweet potato vermicelli. I grab at what looks good, searching for the brands I know. It's all the same, isn't it?

I grab sweet potato candy, dried and sugared, three packages for a dollar. Jars of pickled ginger and garlic, four for a dollar. And tea. All the tea in China, it seems, but it cannot be. Again, which one to pick?

My arms full, I struggle to the cash. I have no hands free to nab moon cakes or rice candy. Next time, next time.

My hands are full as I walk down the street, so many bags dangling at my knees, but there's more. Shaded by a wide umbrella, there's a display of fat juicy lychee, plump and sweet. The man fills a bag of them and directs me inside to pay. There are still so many strange and wondrous fruits I've never tried, afraid I guess, figuring they'll all be as weird and nauseating as durian. Manilla mangos get added to my pile on the counter, and the woman at the cash looks at me approvingly as I juggle my bags to find change for her.

"You like shop Chinatown, yes?"

Yes, yes I do.

# Part 3 – Food Writing

# The Harlem Shuffle

*The Harlem Shuffle - an R&B song originally written and recorded by the duo Bob & Earl in 1963, is named after a line dance step that is an homage to the dance clubs that existed during the Harlem Renaissance of the 1920s. More recently, it refers to the rearranging of plates on a table at Harlem Restaurant when it becomes obvious that too many side dishes have been ordered.*

The term "authentic" gets bandied around a lot these days when it comes to food, with most people not really knowing what the authentic dish should taste like in the first place. So when a commenter on a food-related board dissed the food at Harlem for not being "authentic soul food", I found myself shaking my head.

Harlem soul food is so utterly and totally a product of history. In the early 1900s, African-Americans increasingly migrated north in search of a better standard of living than could be found in the south. They ended up in Harlem, formerly an upscale white neighbourhood, and formed a well-to-do middle class that included the nightclubs, jazz bars, and speakeasies of the 1920s. Southern soul food, which was based on traditional West African dishes with French, Spanish, and Native influences, came with them, but like so many cuisines that are ingredient-based, the dishes changed and morphed from the earthy "make-do" dishes that used gizzards, livers, and chitlins to sophisticated versions of those same foods – less spicy, with more thought to presentation, but with the same basic components. The hearty stick-to-your-ribs quality is what translated in the move from the southern states to Harlem, and what remains prevalent in soul food to this day.

Here in Toronto, owner and chef Carl Cassell has created a little bit of the Harlem Renaissance on Richmond Street East. Although the space opened in March 2007, it seems to have taken a while for people to discover the place, with early accounts on local discussion boards indicating great food but a mostly empty room. The upstairs lounge space has been jumping since day one, however, and Harlem has become one of the hottest reservations in town.

The cozy restaurant is busy when we arrive, but our soft-spoken server is laid back and welcoming. Most hot-ticket places seem more concerned with turning over the tables a couple of times on a Friday night, but no such pressure exists here.

We start with the hummus and avocado dip with Harlem crisps, which turn out to be deep-fried wonton wrappers, and move on to the bourbon baby back ribs appetizer, which is a massive serving of tender pork ribs slathered in a not-too-sweet bourbon-laced sauce, accompanied by a sweet and tangy coleslaw. Across the way, we watch with envy as another table receives the catfish Lafayette, tender morsels of fish in a spicy sauce.

We're not envious long. The jambalaya is full of shrimp, chorizo sausage, scallops. and fat juicy mussels atop al dente rice studded with tomatoes and collard greens. We have collard greens again as one of the many sides we couldn't resist, and they are presented with slivers of red pepper and onion atop a pool of fragrant broth. No sign of the traditional pork hocks, but this may be one of the modernizing touches used in the cuisine.

The fried chicken is the real reason we came and it will be on the table every time we return. The chicken pieces are twice-fried and arrive looking too dark, but one bite reveals a crisp, slightly spicy batter, and moist tender meat inside. Drizzled with a chili-spiked honey, I could happily eat these forever if only my arteries would allow it.

Additional sides in the form of sweet orange candied yams and a warm spicy cornbread studded with corn kernels round out the dinner, with all portions so large that we take half of everything but the chicken home – that didn't last the evening.

For dessert, we opt to share the brownie which comes with a mango sauce and chunks of fresh mango, and is, in a way, the only miss of the evening. While the portion is huge – seriously, it's half a pan of brownies, easily – the cake is dense and slightly tough and way on the sweet side. It fares better the next day, when along with our leftovers, we nuke it for lunch, and the centre warms to a gooey delight.

People often ask me to tell them my favourite restaurant in the city, because they think as a food writer I've got some stash of great places they don't know about. Until now, I've been uncomfortable naming a favourite, but since our visit, I've been answering "Harlem" when that question is put before me. There's a number of reasons for this choice, and the fantastic food and wonderfully professional but unobtrusive service definitely have an influence. But my love of the place also has a lot to do with atmosphere and history.

By recreating the 1920s Harlem renaissance through the combination of music, art and food, Cassell preserves a period in time (important at a time when many of the long-running soul food joints in Harlem, New York, are shutting down) and allows us to experience it (almost) firsthand. Soul food is family food, and Harlem has the uncanny atmosphere of feeling like a family home where Mama is busy in the kitchen cooking up her specialities, and after dinner everyone will head off to a speakeasy to listen to the wail of jazz musicians making history.

# The Sweetest Place on Earth

Some people say Disney is the happiest place on earth. I'd say those people are wrong. I have proof that the happiest place on earth is on Queen Street East, just past the Don River, where Mary Macleod and her small team of bakers make the very best shortbread ever.

Don't believe me? Take James' Beard's word for it – on a visit to Toronto in the early 1980s, the acclaimed chef declared Macleod's shortbread the best he'd ever tasted.

Macleod emigrated to Canada from Scotland in 1955 when she got married. She shares a story of meeting her mother-in-law for the first time: her reputation for being a great cook had preceded her, and her mother-in-law had asked that she bake an apple pie. Not used to the differences in North American flour compared to the softer, more delicate products used in Europe, Macleod's pastry was a disaster, and her embarrassment provoked her to set about researching the different flours and how she could add other natural ingredients to manipulate the dough to work more like the European products she was used to.

She reveals that it took 25 years to perfect the shortbread recipe, passed down from her grandmother, to accommodate the Canadian ingredients.

In 1981, with a marriage broken up and two sons to support, Macleod opened a small shop on Yonge Street at Eglinton Avenue, next door to the Capitol Theatre, which she ran almost entirely on her own. The shop did well but Macleod found her fortune made when a buyer from Holt Renfrew stopped by her shop.

"A beautiful girl in a yellow dress came in and said, 'would you bake for me?'" Macleod recalls with a note of fondness in her voice. That girl walked out with a cookie, but left behind her card.

Macleod processed the Holt's order for delivery in November with the help of a friend. Then word started to spread – Macleod also mentions a write-up in a local paper – and one day in December she discovered people lined up outside her shop. Far more people than she had cookies for.

"I had a friend who ran a restaurant down the street, and I had her give them all coffee and we gave everyone a bit of shortbread, and I said, 'I'll take your names and phone numbers and I'll call you when I have more stock.'"

Those people came back for their shortbread and have returned every year (or more often) and Macleod notes that the children and grandchildren of those original customers are now regulars.

"It was kind of frightening at first because of all the people," she says. "Because in those days I didn't have a mixer or anything, it was all made by hand, so I could only do two pounds of butter at a time."

After the recession of 1992, Macleod came close to losing the business. In addition to the cookie shop, she was running a large restaurant with her son. They had over twenty staff, but overnight the business halted as customers just stopped eating out. She sold her house and moved into a smaller shop in the same Yonge and Eglinton neighbourhood, but it didn't have enough space for all the packing that was necessary for her corporate orders.

She looked for a building for two years and finally, one December, her real estate agent showed up while she was in the process of rolling dough and insisted she check out the Queen Street East building where the business now resides.

The 177-year-old building provides space for Macleod's baking business as well as commercial tenants on the top floors. While the location was considered a bit out of the way when Macleod first set up shop there, the gentrification of the neighbourhood has increased her walk-by traffic. Who can resist the smell of baking shortbread, after all?

While the business has definitely expanded, Macleod and her staff continue to make the cookies out of all-natural ingredients. The small but sun-filled kitchen includes 3 ovens – each can hold 11 sheet pans – and one industrial Hobart mixer. A large table in the centre provides space for packing and decorating the thousands of tins of cookies that will go out over the next few weeks as holiday gifts.

The cookies are a distinctive shape, dropped from a spoon with a domed imprint in the centre, and come in eight flavours. Besides the original shortbread, there is the famous chocolate crunch.

"When I made the chocolate crunch, it took about eighteen months of working on a Saturday night until Sunday morning to come up with the correct amount of butter with the amount of chocolate," Macleod explains. "It's very difficult, no one had ever [mixed chocolate] into pastry before, so I was pretty well the first one in Toronto that I know of that would do that. So I came up with one and I called it chocolate crunch, and everybody loved it."

From the chocolate crunch recipe comes other flavours, including a Dutch crunch, hazelnut, chocolate orange, and chocolate mint. Coffee and coconut shortbread round out the selection in the small, pretty shop at the front of the workspace.

There's also the lesser-known but equally amazing butterscotch shortbread fingers. When I bring some of these home to share with my husband we joke that they might be the key to world domination, they're so impossible to resist.

Touring Macleod's workspace, I am struck by the collection of cookie cutters on display. Besides the flavoured shortbread, Macleod also offers a variety of seasonal holiday cookies, made out of the traditional rolled shortbread.

From bells and trees at Christmas and cute cats and bats for Halloween (no, seriously, the cats are awesome!) to teapots and flowers for Mother's Day and tools for Father's Day, there is something on offer for every holiday. And every holiday becomes a justifiable reason to head to Macleod's shop for a treat.

"I've been very fortunate and grateful that people love it as much as they do because everyone that comes in here, they're always very happy," Macleod says of the many repeat customers.

The products, though, speak for themselves. My own first experience with Macleod's shortbread came about twenty years ago when I was working in an office and a client sent us a tin of cookies at Christmas (50 percent of Macleod's business is corporate orders and the company even designs cookies and packaging with corporate logos). Years before we had the ability to look things up easily on the Internet, I scoured phone books and Perly's map books to find out where this place was so I could have more of these amazing cookies.

Besides the quality products, the other factor that makes Macleod's shop my personal happiest place on earth is its joyfulness. It's impossible to be cranky here. The staff are sweet and friendly and dedicated (one of Macleod's bakers has been with her for 18 years), and everyone who walks through the door is just made to feel so very welcome.

At least a small part of this phenomenon must be attributed to the joy Macleod herself receives from her work. "The feel of the dough is kind of spiritual," she explains, "and I just get a lovely feeling and when I'm making the shortbread. I always think what patience it's got because I've done everything with it and it just works, whatever I want

- like my vision of a cookie, or I'm creating a cookie and it just comes out exactly as I've envisioned it."

For the rest of us, our spiritual experience will come from stopping by the shop and eating one (okay, maybe one more) of Macleod's ethereally good cookies. Sweetest place on earth, people, I'm not kidding.

Sheryl Kirby

# Two Meals

Most of us, if we're lucky, eat three times a day – or more. We can look at this activity as either a chore, or a joy. We can take pleasure in every flavour, every spice, every texture, and every smell, or we can look at eating as something we have to do to stay alive – but man, doesn't that get tedious after a while?

Recently, I had the opportunity to experience both ends of the spectrum.

April 2009 marked the twentieth anniversary of the last time I had eaten at McDonald's. I wanted to mark the occasion in some way, but none of the options was appealing – especially the ones that might get me arrested. Instead I chose to do the most radical thing I could think of, which was to go and eat a meal at McDonald's. Heck, I've eaten bull's testicles, it couldn't be that bad, could it? And to counter the

McDonald's meal, a few days later I would be attending the Slow Food Banchetto feast, a five-course meal created by 25 of Toronto's top chefs. Since the Slow Food movement was created in 1986 in response to the opening of a McDonald's near the Spanish Steps in Rome, it seemed like a reasonable way to mark the anniversary.

The McDonald's meal, as expected, was disgusting. The burgers were greyish brown and had the spongy texture of crepe soles on a pair of shoes. The McChicken sandwich was bland and beige and resembled a flat disc of breaded particleboard (which, considering how mechanically deboned chicken is actually made, would have been more palatable). The fries smelled and tasted of rancid grease. The fruit pies were spit out and thrown away, they were so soggy and bland. The first few bites of the meal took me hurtling back to 1989, when this was something I would have described as delicious, but my grown-up self could not stomach that food or the hard seats, bright lights, chaotic service area, or the aura of sadness and defeat that permeated the restaurant.

Later that week, I joined two hundred others for five courses of Canadian-focused food, dishes that featured charcuterie, local trout, bread and biscuits made from red fife flour, fiddleheads, wild leeks, maple syrup, BC stinging nettles, Tamworth pig, local honey, and a selection of Ontario wines. There was an enthusiasm in the air – Slow Food Founder and President Carlo Petrini was the guest of honour — but it was also obvious that the guests in attendance were excited about the food.

Petrini spoke enthusiastically to the crowd about real gastronomy, about enjoying the food we eat and about the importance of protecting regional cuisines, local ingredients, and traditional preparations. He referred to the University of Grandmothers, encouraging us to go back to past generations and learn from them in order to keep traditional foodways alive.

The contrast with the McDonald's meal was obvious, and in so many ways these meals represent the two extremes in our society.

Price, of course is the most obvious: dinner for two at McDonald's was under 12 dollars, dinner for two at the Slow Food Banchetto was 300 dollars. To be fair, the event was for charity, and was most definitely a special occasion. I would hope that most people don't eat this much rich, fatty food on a daily basis – it was a pulling-out-all-the-stops event that, while fun, was an obvious extreme.

Also, the emphasis on quality cannot be overlooked. While the food at McDonald's might fill the hungry hole or bribe a screaming child into submission, no one is pretending that it's good for us (in fact, the opposite has been well documented) or the environment. The McDonald's I visited didn't even offer recycling bins for garbage. The Slow Food menu, however, was created from locally grown produce, foraged foods, and rare-breed pigs.

It could be argued that the world has flip-flopped. The Slow Food meal we ate comprising foraged foods and charcuterie made from the less popular bits of animals was once the food of the poor, while the poor now eat out-of-season food grown with cheap labour in other countries. In a time when people are losing their homes and the resources at food banks are stretched, it's unfair to wag a finger and lecture them about eating better-quality food, but I can also understand Petrini's insistence that an appreciation of good food is vital to our society.

Critics have accused the Slow Food movement of being cult-like, and of being both elitist and self-congratulatory regarding their efforts to encourage the consumption of "good, clean, fair food". I didn't get that vibe from Petrini (and I'm a consummate cynic); rather, I saw a man who cares deeply about an issue that has worldwide significance.

A couple of speakers at the Banchetto dinner did, unfortunately, perpetuate the image of elitism and self-congratulations. At one point, everyone in the room who had attended Terra Madre (a Slow Food event held in Torino, Italy every two years) was asked to stand and be acknowledged for their contribution to promoting the principles of Slow Food, while the rest of us sat by feeling oddly uncomfortable – were we supposed to be applauding these folks because they could afford a plane ticket to Italy? The MC for the event acknowledged the contribution of specific food writers in the room who had helped to promote the event, but not all of them. These actions, while perhaps unconscious and unintended, separated the crowd, which included the paying public along with Slow Food organizers and delegates, into A- and B-list guests.

Social faux pas aside, the principles of the movement are sound and logical. What needs to happen now is a shift in which people who would normally turn to those dry grey burgers at McDonald's or other fast food chains look to factors other than cost when choosing what to eat. I'm not suggesting replacing 10 dollars worth of fast food with a 150 dollar per plate feast – that's unrealistic even for the well-to-do. But given that I could make the meal I had at McDonald's from scratch for the same price or less using fresh, local, and sustainable ingredients, and have a far healthier meal on my plate when I sit down to eat, Petrini's suggestion of getting back to basics, or home cooking with simple quality ingredients, doesn't seem too out of whack.

Meeting in the middle between the two extremes requires a societal shift, however. It means reassessing priorities, such as how we spend our free time. It means putting the whole family to work helping to prepare meals. It means placing value on quality over cost, eating with the seasons, and choosing to support local farmers. It also means beginning to think of food as a pleasure, to look at a beautiful (and lovingly prepared) dinner as a reward at the end of the day, instead of thinking of food as mere fuel, or food preparation as a chore.

My McDonald's meal was a sad experience in a depressing place that left me feeling dirty and unhappy. It wasn't the joyful, fun experience the clown in the commercials made it out to be at all. And while some in the Slow Food movement may require a slight adjustment of attitude and perception if they really want their organization to grow and be accepted by the mainstream, I firmly believe that their hearts are in the right place and that the foundations of the movement's philosophy come from wanting the best for the world – for the earth, for the farmers, and for the co-producers who eat the final products.

Who do you think McDonald's is rooting for?

# Apple Pissybeds

Having learned to cook at the side of my grandmother, I was startled to learn in my own middle age that this same grandmother, who has been responsible for preparing three meals a day, for a varying number of hungry mouths, for the past seventy years, actually hates to cook. My cousin and I always assumed that the things she let us do while helping her prepare food were meant to be fun. For us. As it turns out they were often ways for her to make the process more interesting for herself, and if she was able to take a shortcut or two in the name of "fun", then all the better.

The "pissybed" is really just a free-form pie. In France, it would fall under the header of "galette" if galette meant "Shit, my pastry is crap today and isn't going to roll out properly!" Because this kind of pie is usually what you end up with, albeit unintentionally, if your pie crust is crap. You can make pissybeds if your pie crust is fine, as is my grandmother's, but know that unless they get to taste it, people will think you've made them because your dough is a mess. My grandma wouldn't know a galette from a whosit – there weren't a lot of fancy French people in rural Nova Scotia. Well, there were, once, but the English shipped them off to Louisiana to become Cajuns.

In any case, the name "pissybed" is not some French derivative, but rather a name that came about because, according to my grandma, the pie looks like the bundle of wet sheets you end up with when one of your kids pees the bed in the middle of the night. Helen Kirby clearly missed her calling as a stand-up comedienne.

My grandma makes pissybeds as a whole pie, usually on a flat baking sheet. Because I tend to make pies in a smaller version (just two of us to feed versus my grandma's houseful of six or seven people) I use 6-inch pie pans, but the point of a free-form pie is that you can make it however you like.

I use lard in my crust and half red fife whole wheat flour, and the apples are a mix of Empires, Gingergolds, and Sunrises with plenty of cinnamon, nutmeg, ginger, and a pinch of allspice, plus sugar, a bit of flour and plenty of butter. Milk and sugar brushed on in the last ten minutes of baking makes for a crunchy crust. Pisybeds are not intended to be pretty – which is definitely where they stray from a galette, where the crust is usually crimped in an attractive manner, and the fruit is artistically arranged – the deal is to just encase those apples in pastry, mush it all together and let it be ugly, but delicious.

Sheryl Kirby

# The Rustic Rut

Do you know this man in the plaid shirt, suspenders, and toque, wielding an axe? Have you seen him recently in a food service capacity, either as a server or a chef/cook? Or possibly making your morning coffee? Do you live in a backwoods logging camp, hundreds of miles from the nearest town? Because that's the only reason why we should be eating food served and prepared by lumberjacks. No, really, take another look at him. Minus the axe, he could pass for any Toronto barista, hipster server, or chef at a place that serves "rustic" fare.

Yes, yet another "rustic" Italian restaurant is opening in Toronto (four since the beginning of 2010). We're still desperately trying to find more things to put on poutine. Late night comfort food now has its own cross-border trend: "stoner haute cuisine" for the after-club crowd (back in my day, all we had at 2am were donairs, and we were happy to have it! /end old geezer Haligonian rant). And while all those things are good and tasty – I can't possibly be the only person longing for a little bit of elegance and sophistication on my plate occasionally.

This rustic comfort food thing – it made sense two or three years ago in 2008, when a recession loomed over our heads. The world was a scary place, high-end restaurants were shutting down with some regularity, and we just wanted something familiar on the plates in front of us. Nonna's spaghetti, plenty of fries, some "of the people" pulled pork, piles of game meat to assuage our inner wannabe hunter, and bacon on every damned thing in sight. Like our pioneer forefathers and mothers, we ate all the parts of the animal, preferably served on a cross-section of log, complete with bark around the outside. We canned and pickled and imagined ourselves as a modern day Laura Ingalls (or Catherine Parr Trail if you want to keep it local and Canadian). We lumbered through the spring growth of local woodlands stomping down (or over-harvesting) the very jewels of the forest we claimed to prize and revere. We rejected anything that wasn't "local", which meant we ate an awful lot of "white people food", in the process making many immigrant citizens feel that their cuisine was second class.

Don't get me wrong, it's all been very tasty. And homey and comforting and… rustic. But man, isn't it getting boring? Roast chicken, mashed potatoes, mac and cheese, pulled pork, Sunday roast, charcuterie plates – on every damn menu in the city. They're becoming interchangeable. Likewise for that rustic Italian stuff. Again, it's all good, perfected to taste just like what Mama might make at home. But that begs the question – why aren't we just eating it at home?

I ordered roast chicken in a restaurant the other night. It was great – no complaints. But I roasted a chicken at home last week that was just as good. Same goes for mac and cheese. Why am I ordering food at restaurants that I can make at home, where it costs less and often tastes better? Sure, not everyone can cook, and everyone is comforted by rustic comfort food. But remember when going out to a restaurant was a reason to try something new and exciting? To dress up? When you tried not to look like a lumberjack? When you took your goddamned hat off?

Remember when food was art, and drama? When chefs took risks instead of playing it safe by cooking food that you'd eat at home? I'm not talking about our short, sad romance with molecular gastronomy, but a time when chefs were actually trying to make the experience of eating out something sophisticated. A beautiful room, professionally trained servers who melted into the background but were ever at the ready, food that was breath-taking to look at and mind-blowing to eat because the chef had taken risks and played with flavours and pushed boundaries.

I'm not suggesting we bring back "tall food". I don't want silly fronds on every plate like weird green antennae. I just want to be able to go out and have a meal that I wouldn't have eaten at home when I was eight years old. I want a reason to dress up instead of feeling like I'm overdressed because my server is wearing Converse sneakers and a toque that stinks of dirty hair.

I want new restaurants to stop working from the same menu playbooks as the last twenty restaurants that opened in this city and do something different and interesting. I want more restaurants from under-appreciated cultures (Kenyan food, Peruvian cuisine, true Persian food as opposed to generic "Middle Eastern") instead of yet another menu full of "look at us, we cook local!" Canadiana clichés. Because it's all becoming a cliché.

Our country cruised through the recession. For most of us, things are good. We're welcoming hundreds of thousands of new citizens to our country every year. Yet most of our city's top restaurants are serving the same damned (white people food) dishes based on what people were eating in this country two hundred years ago. It's gotten to the point where I wouldn't be surprised to see bannock on a rustic, local restaurant menu.

Chefs of Toronto – I am not a lumberjack. Please stop making me eat like one!

*Since writing and publishing this piece in early 2010 on the now-defunct website TasteTO.com, no less than three restaurants have opened in Toronto serving some form of bannock. I should take up fortune-telling.*

# Assessing the Haggis

After putting together a round up of Robert Burns Day activities and dinners, I was just about haggissed out. Then Chef Martin Kouprie of Pangaea Restaurant sent me a message on Twitter. He was holding a haggis competition for his kitchen staff; the winning dish would be served in the restaurant on Robert Burns Day. Would I like to come and be a judge?

I was of two minds; my experience with offal – all organs and all animals (I've only recently learned to like foie gras) – hasn't been good. But then I remembered the advice of Vogue food writer Jeffrey Steingarten, that you must try a food at least ten times before you can determine that you truly don't like it. I'd had haggis once before and found it repulsive, but here was an opportunity to try seven additional versions of the dish, created by seven different professional cooks who would be pulling out all the stops to make the lowly stuffed sheep's stomach into gourmet fare.

On the big day, we gathered together at a large table at the back of Pangaea. Besides myself and Chef Kouprie, the judges included Toronto Star food writer Corey Mintz, chef and cookbook author Lucy Waverman, and Alison Fryer of The Cookbook Store.

Waverman and Fryer, both of Scottish descent, had one over on the rest of us as they were both connoisseurs of haggis, having eaten it growing up. They had a better scope of what makes a good versus a bad haggis (balance of spices; ratio of offal – generally heart, lungs and liver, aka the "pluck"; consistency; and texture of the casing) and both based their assessment on the haggis themselves (note, the plural of "haggis" is, in fact, "haggis", although we were unsure at the time and considered both "haggises" and "haggi"), whereas the rest of us looked more to the whole dish.

Of the seven dishes presented, only one was served in an actual sheep's stomach. Which was fine by all of us, since the sheep's stomach was much thicker than the intestines and artificial casings used in the other dishes and added its own distinct flavour to an already strong filling. Besides the pluck, haggis are typically stuffed with pinhead oatmeal or pearl barley, onions, suet, spices, and salt, with the whole thing being left to simmer for a few hours until the filling is cooked. I know, it just gets more and more appetizing.

The haggis ranged from mild in flavour to very strong and offally. One version, presented as a meat pie in a parmesan pastry crust and topped with beet relish, was the least authentic haggis-wise, but was the most palatable to me because it was also the one that tasted the least of the pluck. Another version that I could live with, and potentially enjoy, was a deep-fried version in which balls of the haggis filling were dipped in batter and fried. There was much discussion at the judging table, particularly by Waverman and Fryer, as to the complete inauthenticity of this version, but a Google search after the fact reveals that it's a regular offering in Scottish fish and chip shops, served up either as a burger patty or in balls with tomato relish.

Accompaniments were where the competitors really shone, and

where the winning dish edged out the others. Many versions of neeps and tatties (turnips or rutabagas and potatoes, generally mashed) appeared before us, some liberally flavoured with horseradish, others topped with fried leeks and slices of candied parsnip. One entry offered amazingly light crepe-like potato pancakes, while the deep-fried haggis came with crisp spicy fries.

The winning dish, however, as created by saucier Christopher Waye, took haggis into gourmet territory. Waye's dish offered two small rounds of a mild sausage-shaped haggis, served atop diced turnips, chanterelle mushrooms, caramelized Brussels sprouts, and garnished with a poached egg. Waye's reasoning for the egg was that it essentially created its own sauce, giving the diner something to dip the haggis into.

As the haggis-hater of the group, I definitely appreciated this consideration – anything available on the plate to eat with the haggis and thus mask some of what I came to refer to as the "stank of death" from the offal was A-okay by me. Fryer and Waverman took umbrage with the inclusion of the chanterelles, citing them as unnecessary and claiming that they unbalanced the dish. This is true to some extent, but hey, it's chanterelles. I'll take yours if you don't want 'em.

Waye's haggis dish will be offered on Pangaea's lunch menu on Robert Burns Day. For his efforts, the saucier was presented with a bottle of The Macallan 17 Year Old whisky, which he undoubtedly was expected to share with his co-workers in the back of house.

And while I didn't learn to love that "Great Chieftain o' the Pudding Race", I came quite a bit closer to my "ten tries" and knowing that I probably don't like haggis all that much. Waye most definitely made it palatable (although I will admit to eating only one slice of the haggis and concentrating on the other delights on the plate), and I'd recommend that anyone who is haggis-curious go check out his dish as it's certainly a more elegant and accessible one than the traditional serving suggestion.

Sheryl Kirby

# The Life-Changing Mole

**I** am befuddled by people who don't like food. It's partially why I hate the term "foodie" so much – who doesn't like food? Who among us isn't a "foodie"? But I guess it's fair to note that some of us care a bit more than others. Not just fuel to keep us alive, food is beauty and art and love, all rolled into one. A perfect meal can be as emotional as a first kiss or a last goodbye.

Which is why I found myself sitting in Frida Restaurant, barely able to hold back the well of tears.

Having just eaten what might possibly be one of the best meals of my life, I found myself clinging to Chef Pilar Cabrera Arroyo's hand, unable to let go, uttering "thank you" over and over again.

Yes, I'd had a fair amount to drink, including a gourd of mescal, but the sheer brilliance of Cabrera's thirty-ingredient authentic Oaxacan mole will likely remain one of the highlights of my food writing career.

Cabrera was in town for the month of September 2009 to cook dinners at a variety of Toronto restaurants including the dinner I attended at Frida as well as Veritas, Torito, FRANK, The Chef's House, and a demo at Nella Cucina.

A native of Oaxaca, Cabrera is the owner and chef of the award-winning restaurant La Olla (The Pot). She also runs a cooking school called Casa de los Sabores (House of Flavours) where she teaches others the many dishes of the Oaxacan region that have been passed down through her family. A noted student is US chef Rick Bayless, known for his restaurants featuring authentic Mexican cuisine.

Her trip to Toronto was organized by Alvin Starkman, an ex-pat Torontonian who now runs a bed and breakfast in the Oaxacan region. Food writer Mary Luz Mejia curated the events, arranging for Chef Cabrera to team up with some of Toronto's best-known chefs for a series of dinners that showcase the famous dishes of the southern Mexican state.

While Cabrera brought some ingredients with her, such as epazote and the black mole paste required for the famous mole negro, she was impressed with the availability of authentic Mexican ingredients in Toronto. Her hosts took her to Kensington Market where she visited the South American markets on Augusta Avenue and was duly impressed with shops like Perolas.

During the dinner at Frida, Cabrera tag-teamed with Frida's Chef Jose Hadad, taking turns on the dishes in this magnificent six-course meal. The two chefs presented a corn soup, salad with cactus paddles, grilled shrimp with mango and chili salsa, steamed tamal with lamb, and Cabrera's mole atop turkey medallions stuffed with plaintain. A Mexican goat's milk cheesecake and truly fantastic churros made for a memorable dessert (the churros were from Chef Hadad at Frida, and are probably the best in the city – we'll definitely be going back for more of these!).

For those unfamiliar with the term, mole can be any kind of sauce, and the Oaxaca region is famously known as the Land of Seven Moles.

Because the area is in the south and has remained relatively secluded, the food has maintained its authenticity – there are no nachos or hard taco shells to be found here, although the influence of the Spanish can be seen in the variety of spices.

The mole negro is the most famous of the Oaxacan moles and typically contains twenty to thirty ingredients, including chocolate, chili, onions, garlic, nuts, and spices. It is normally made in the morning and left to simmer all day so the flavours blend and meld into a thick, rich, almost black sauce so intense and flavourful it can bring tears of happiness to the eyes of anyone who eats it.

Lest I give the impression that Hadad and Cabrera fed us rustic food, it should be noted that this is an extremely elegant cuisine, with a very natural but sophisticated presentation and intriguing flavour profiles. The heat of the chilies in many dishes never overwhelmed but built from almost nothing to a comfortable warmth. Balances of sweet, salty and acidic were quite precise, making it all seem simple, although as anyone who has tried to make a dish like mole will know – it's about more than throwing the right ingredients into a pot.

Cooking a perfect mole is part art, part skill, part devoted attention to detail, and much love. Eating that same perfect mole is an ethereal experience that every person should have at least once in their lifetime. Like rainbows, rare birds, and family milestones, opportunities like this don't come along very often.

# Stress Cooking

If there is one phrase, one turn of words that is guaranteed to drive me insane, it is the well-intentioned but patronizing assurance that "there's nothing you can do about it, so there's no point in worrying". Again, I know that the phrase is delivered with good intentions, as a way to help the person in question stop worrying and calm down. But in a genuinely dire or horrific situation, who among us is able to quiet our minds and turn our attention to something else? It's possible, but not easy, and if you're a type A control freak, it's damned near impossible. Situations in which there is nothing I can do are exactly when I worry the most, because I am helpless to create a positive outcome. It's why people are sent off to boil water when a woman goes into labour – it gives them something to do to keep them from being underfoot and lets them think they're helping in some way.

In the stressful situations in which there is nothing I can do to achieve a positive outcome (which, by the above theory, makes me even more stressed), I cook. Lots. Mass quantities of things – restaurant quantities – just to keep my hands and mind busy, so that I might, for a short while, stop worrying. It seldom stops the worrying completely, the issue is still there at the back of my head, throbbing like a migraine dulled by pain medicine but not completely cured. But at least I'm not just sitting there fussing. At least there's something to show for my nervous energy.

Back in my concert production days, I'd manage my way through the lead-up to shows by cooking. In 1998, when we presented Convergence and had five hundred people from all over the world coming in to Toronto for the weekend, Greg and I threw a barbeque in our backyard as a pre-festival party for the bands and selected guests. This was less of a huge gesture of hospitality and more of a way to find people to eat the mass quantities of food that I was churning out in the days before the event as I waited to see which bands cleared customs, and whether the venues were able to meet our technical specs, or if I was going to have to find a legal pyrotechnic set-up at the eleventh hour (and does our insurance even cover pyrotechnics?!).

I cooked with a kitchen full of rock stars gathered around the table behind me. I stacked bowls of salads and piles of cheesecakes on top of gear boxes full of drum kits and synthesizers. When it became overwhelming I sent the lot of them, in all their goth finery, to the store with a list of items that I needed to finish dinner.

A year later, at another weekend-long music festival, we ditched the paid caterers used to fulfil the bands' hospitality riders and I cooked band meals for twenty or thirty people each night for three nights in a row. I'd have been doing it anyway – might as well put my stress cooking to good use.

These days, I'm stress cooking again. Once more I find myself with no choice but to sit and wait and accept what fate hands me, with no ability to step in and have an effect on the final outcome.

Four weeks ago, Greg and I stood helplessly by and watched our 11-year-old dog collapse and die on the kitchen floor. It was fast and painless, but totally unexpected, and the shock has thrown us for a loop. Just as we started to come to terms with this reality, a relative was admitted to the palliative care ward in his fight against cancer. The details are being taken care of by other family members, so all we can do is sit and wait – for days, maybe weeks – but there is nothing we can do, either to ease his suffering or to help put his affairs in order.

So to fill the time, I cook. Big pots of soup, three different kinds today. Packed into containers and into the freezer, a wall of beets, curried parsnips, corn chowder, built solid and frozen to keep the bad things at bay and comfort us in our times of sorrow. Quick and easy, but also familiar and soothing, meals to have ready when the other relatives arrive and need sustenance to deal with their long journey and their grief.

Christmas cookies, tray after tray, mocking in their festive cheerfulness, but life goes on, traditions continue, even with the aching gaps once filled by those we love and have lost. This is what we really mean by the term "comfort food": the things with fond memories attached that ease our emotional distress by reminding us that, as much as things change, they stay the same. It's maybe not such a great idea to fill an emotional void with food, but in times of stress, eating – and cooking – might be the only thing that keeps us on an even keel.

At the end of the day, after the soup has been packed away, the dishes washed, the cookies decorated and frozen for gift baskets, the stress is still there. It comes flooding back – in good times, as a mental checklist of things that must be done, or excitement at the coming event; in bad times as a reverberating sense of loss. An aching back, sore feet, a new callous, or a small burn from some splattering soup distract for a bit longer. Maybe there's some acceptance of the situation in the waves of exhaustion, or just some thankfulness at having made it through a few hours with something to show for it. The mind still races – what can I cook tomorrow? A shopping list forms, a game of mental Tetris at the calculations of how many more batches of cookies will fit in an already-full freezer, or whether any of the soon-to-be-visiting relatives are vegetarian.

Wait. Worry. Cook. Ad infinitum.

Sheryl Kirby

# Cupcakes for Daniel

I can't remember the last time I baked anything from a mix. My husband, Greg, had a passing fancy with a disappointing Boston cream pie mix at one point in 2005 when I had a broken arm and he was attempting to do some of the cooking, but it was a sad affair that we agreed never to repeat.

Besides usually being not very good, cake mixes have the uncanny ability to suck absolutely all the fun out of baking. Dump powder, add water or milk, stir. Meh. I get that this is exactly the amount of effort that is desired by people who do not like to bake but for some reason want to "make a cake", instead of going out to a nice bakery and buying something professional. But for those of us who dig the process of baking, cake mixes are not a lot of fun.

Which is why this particular box of cake mix is such a conundrum.

When Greg's uncle Daniel passed away at the end of November 2010 (as a single man with no partner and no kids) he left an apartment full of stuff that needed to be dealt with. Daniel wasn't a hoarder, but he definitely had some pack-rat tendencies, and his tiny little apartment often felt like a delicate dollhouse to my lumbering built-like-a-brick-shithouse frame, a situation exacerbated by the fact that there was so much stuff everywhere.

As Daniel spent most of his adult life working as a chef, much of what he collected was food-related. Every time I saw him, he gifted me with cookbooks, or baking pans, or little gadgets and utensils. Many of these he'd pick up at thrift shops and yard sales, treasures that he couldn't pass up but likely knew he'd never need.

After he passed away, we went to his apartment to help pack up his belongings. Two of Greg's other uncles were there, as well as Daniel's landlady and an upstairs neighbour he was friends with. Much of the food in the fridge and cupboards had already been removed – the landlady and the neighbour, Serge, who was training to be a chef himself, had cleaned out the kitchen when Daniel was moved to the palliative care ward a few weeks earlier. But in a small back room, we found a whole stash of cookware – pans, utensils, plastic containers – and a shelf full of dry goods including bags of rice, crackers, tubs of flours and grains, and oddly, a selection of cake mixes.

We all stood in wonderment and looked at the brightly coloured boxes like they were some foreign object we'd never seen before. This was Daniel, who loved to bake probably more than anything else, who made a killing every Christmas selling his famous fruitcake to friends and acquaintances. What the hell would Daniel be doing with cake mixes?

Serge the neighbour took most of the boxes. He might be a chef-in-training, but he was also a starving student. But I nabbed the confetti angel food cake. I'm not sure why – the package was expired, and I don't even own a bundt pan. Maybe it dated back to my childhood when my very favourite cake, and the one I asked for at every birthday, was a confetti cake with pink icing. It was something about the rainbow hues of the sprinkles – so much cooler than brown chocolate.

(To this day, chocolate cake is usually the last thing I'll order off a dessert menu.)

My plan had been to make the cake and take it to the funeral – those rainbow sprinkles would have been perfect with the rainbow flag placed on the altar with Daniel's chef apron and the urn containing his ashes. But those days were busy, and stressful, and the holidays were fast approaching and I just didn't get it done. So after Christmas, after all the cake and cookies and candies were gone, I pulled out the cake mix and whipped it up.

I made cupcakes for lack of a bundt pan. Then to cover up the vaguely chemical taste of the cake (I nearly had a heart attack when I read the ingredients on the label), I made a rich butter cream, tinted it pink, and spread a thick layer on each cupcake. Of course, being light and airy angel food, the cakes were at risk of collapse from the weight of the frosting, but it didn't matter. I added some colourful sprinkles and they were done.

They were, well… they were gay. In the best sense of the word. Sweet and light and pink with rainbow sprinkles inside and out. They were me when I was seven and adored everything pink. They were the raucous joy of a Pride parade on a glorious summer day, and they were Daniel, singing, pirouetting in his kitchen, and filling our pockets with candy as Greg and I left his house after an evening spent together.

I regret not getting them made for the funeral. All of Daniel's friends would have totally appreciated how much the cupcakes represented him, from the rainbow sprinkles to the sharing of food, something that Daniel loved to do. We didn't eat them all ourselves; I sent them off to work with Greg to share with his co-workers, which felt like the most important part of the process.

I'm sure Daniel didn't leave that cake mix there on purpose for us to find. He was too sick near the end to do much planning or organizing, and that back room was a treasure trove of goodies and oddities. But he obviously bought that box with the intention of making that cake at some point. To honour a man who helped shape my love of food and cooking, making that cake was the least that I could do.

# Local Yokels

Allow me to play devil's advocate for a moment.

I had a conversation with a colleague recently in which the subject turned to local food. Specifically, how people in the Toronto area are prone to blindly follow and buy anything grown locally despite the quality of the products themselves.

My colleague suggested that most consumers want their farmers' markets to carry the same things that the grocery stores do (instead of the other way around) – i.e. varieties of fruits and vegetables similar to the bland varieties grown in California that were mostly developed for easy shipping. My colleague also suggested that certain local food producers create products of inferior quality; that many esteemed Toronto chefs who specialize in local food don't actually offer a good quality meal; and that fans of local food willingly buy these inferior products or meals anyway because they refuse to acknowledge their own sense of taste, instead deferring to local "experts" or advocates (chefs, food writers, etc.) who tell the food-lovers what to like and what to buy.

I don't necessarily agree with all of this opinion, thus my "devil's advocate" disclaimer – please don't shoot the messenger – but on some levels, my colleague has a point. The argument cooked in my head a bit, because I've been wondering for a while. How many local products are we buying because they're the best products available, and how much of it is for the ideology of "supporting local"?

The first thing to take note of here is that Toronto is really quite progressive when it comes to supporting local food artisans. In terms of any kind of "food identity", it's a defining feature of our food scene. We herald our chefs who support local producers, and know the names of our farmers.

Not everyone agrees with the premise, of course. When running TasteTO.com, I had writers who bristled when they were told they couldn't write a review of a restaurant in another country – it's called TasteTO, our mandate is pretty clear – and the reply I got, that Toronto doesn't have any high-quality restaurants, was both shocking and frustrating. In that typical Canadian lack-of-self-esteem kind of way, we sell ourselves short on the world stage because there are no Michelin stars sparkling in our towns.

And maybe it's that lack of self-esteem that caused our food scene to latch onto the local movement so devotedly. Toronto measures itself against other places so obsessively that having something to call our own – like a local food movement in a city surrounded by some of the best agricultural land in the world – seems like an honour no one can take from us. And as with every other social movement or trend (be it in music or art or theatre) Toronto may be late to the game, but once we hop on the bandwagon we don't do things in half measures. So when local became the big buzzword, we went all in.

Which is fantastic (remember, devil's advocate here). And gives us a unique food identity. Paris may be posh and high-end, New York may have all that awesome street food, but in Toronto, we've got at least one accessible farmers' market every single day of the week. We've got people willing to invest in local food artisans. We've got a plethora of restaurants all dedicated to serving locally grown food and to working with specific farms. In fact, I saw a comment by a food blogger recently about a new restaurant opening, in which they were disappointed that this place didn't seem to have any kind of policy for serving local food. We are at the point where we expect such a policy to be in place, regardless of the nature of the restaurant, and where a lack of such a policy might just be business suicide.

Which brings me back to my colleague's comment. Because what if that newly opened restaurant chose to source its products from non-local producers because it believed the quality was better? I'll give you a moment to be aghast and curse the place out. But then let's get back to the meat of the question.

Winemakers use the theory of terroir to determine which grapes should be grown where. Soil, weather, and general growing conditions all determine whether a wine will taste good or bad. For instance, syrahs grown in warm regions are preferable to those grown in cooler areas. Using the same theory, wouldn't it make sense that a peach grown in Georgia might actually taste better than a peach grown in Ontario? Or that blueberries grown in Nova Scotia taste better than those grown here?

I know, it feels blasphemous to even type it. But while I'll happily eat Ontario blueberries, I can immediately tell the difference between local berries and those "from away", specifically from the Maritimes where the salt air and scrappy topsoil barely attached to the granite bedrock make for a distinct flavour that is almost umami-like in character. And my preference (sorry) is for the blueberries from Nova Scotia. Even if they're cultivated. I'll surely take Ontario berries over something imported from the US or Chile, but I know my own tastes enough to realize that, for me, the Ontario product is a far second place.

But does everybody supporting the local food scene have the same sense of their own tastes? Heck, do they even know that it's okay to stand up and say it out loud? My colleague doesn't think they do.

Despite wanting to support farmers' markets and eat locally, most people still want their produce to be perfect and unblemished like it is in the grocery stores. Most of us don't challenge our farmers to grow more flavourful varieties better suited to our climate because we want stuff to be consistent.

Don't believe me? Okay, besides Bing, name a variety of cherry (and no, maraschino does not count!). Odds are, most people can't do it without using their Google-fu. And most people wouldn't know the difference, flavour-wise.

The bigger question though, is: Why is it like this? We're all interested in supporting local producers, artisans, chefs and farmers – not just for environmental reasons or to bolster our food identity, but to actually support our own communities. So why haven't we taken the time to know the products that we're buying, or determine our own tastes? I know that most of us really do believe in supporting local food, and we do what we can by shopping at farmers' markets and shops that sell local products, as well as eating at restaurants that serve local food. But we're taking what is being handed to us and not asking questions. Sure, we eat local, but we don't know local. Which kind of makes the whole exercise a bit pointless.

The initial debate stemmed from a feeling that people just can't be bothered. I want to believe that's not the case, that my colleague is even more cynical than I am. Because most of us wouldn't make the effort to go to market, to visit restaurants, to spend extra on local food if we didn't care. Just as supporting local food producers takes effort, it also takes effort to learn more about the food we eat. Simply going to market isn't enough. We need to build a partnership that ensures local farmers are growing the best, most flavourful varieties that work best within our growing conditions. And maybe we need to accept that some things will just taste better coming from somewhere else.

Consumers

- Know your farmer. And that whole "get to know your farmer" bit is about more than "nice weather we're having, eh,

Farmer Brown?" If the farmers you buy from at markets don't identify their produce by variety, ask them. Ask about the difference. If they do offer more than one variety of something, ask for samples. It's got to be about more than lip service to the ideology – we've all got to be more proactive.

- Attend events that teach about varieties of certain foods so you can learn the differences between them.
- Taste every darn (food) thing you can get into your mouth. If your memory is poor, keep a tasting notebook like beer and wine geeks do.
- Be not afraid of the naked emperor. You're entitled to your own sense of taste and your own opinions on local products. You don't have to like something just because every other foodie is fawning over it. Dissenting voices not only make for great debate, but also foster change. The farmer/chef/artisan might even take your (constructive) criticism to heart and work to improve their product because of it.

Chefs and Restaurateurs

- By all means support local producers, but remember that discerning diners are also looking for quality. Don't think that by holding up that "local food" sign we'll forgive a bad meal.
- Use your menus to explain varieties or breeds chosen for your menu; use your floor staff to explain your choice of variety. Get everyone involved in the educational aspect of the meal.
- Embrace your role of food advocate and consider tasting menus or dishes that showcase different varieties of a specific product to help teach diners about what's available.
- Hold dinners and events that feature local farmers and producers – and price them reasonably so not just the well-to-do food snobs can attend.

Farmers, Shops and Stores

- Label your produce by varietal so customers can get to know the differences. Apples come in more kinds than red, green, and yellow.
- Where possible, offer samples or hold comparative tastings of in-season produce.
- Offer printed literature on seasonal ingredients and varieties, encouraging customers to try more obscure varieties.
- Make an effort to grow (or carry) obscure items so customers can expand their palates.
- Grow what tastes the best, whether in terms of variety or knowing that something just doesn't match the terroir.

# Why Local Needs to Go Mass Market

I bought asparagus at the supermarket today.

I know. Step aside so the vigilante hordes of locavores can get past in order to more easily place my head on a pike.

It was local, if that makes any difference.

I know. I should still be supporting the farmers at farmers' markets. More of the money goes directly to the farmers than if I buy local produce at Price Chopper.

But you know what? Maybe we need to think about purchasing local in a different way. See, when the produce manager pulled that bunch of asparagus out of the box, he had a little gleam in his eye. He knew it was good stuff. Perfectly sized, tight heads, bright green. We looked down at the asparagus, then back up at each other. "Heh?" he said, smiling. "Gimme it," was my reply.

Here's my theory on this issue: Yes, more money goes directly to the farmer if we buy our produce directly from the farmer. But despite the fact that Toronto's got farmers' markets every day of the week, and piles of CSAs, they're not always convenient to get to. Those of us "in the bubble" make the effort to get there. But we're the minority. Everyone else is all about the one-stop-shopping. So if we want more people to eat locally grown food, we have to accept that some of them are going to do it at the supermarket.

The problem is that supermarkets are ginormous corporations that work on economy of scale. One of the arguments given by the chains for not carrying more local strawberries is that they have chain-wide contracts with California growers that they're not able to ditch during the small window when local berries come into season. And since they can't risk losing these contracts (because even though they're gross, consumers have become accustomed to having strawberries in January), they have to go with the bigger supplier.

Where am I going with this? Well, as much as I believe in supporting local farmers, I'm also of the opinion that the only way to spread the word about local produce is to make it more available to the average consumer. Which means it has to be in the supermarkets. Farmers may make less per unit, but they're also saving the time and effort and the related cost of travelling to market in the first place.

More importantly, buying local produce (or organic, etc.) in a supermarket sends a message. Every sku scanned is tabulated. Price Chopper knows exactly how many units of local asparagus it's selling. If it doesn't sell well (because we're all out buying it at markets) then they'll stop carrying it. So at the very least, we need to make sure that these stores see an interest in local products and continue to carry them so that other shoppers (who don't normally shop at farmers' markets) will see those products and have the opportunity to buy them.

Let's look at eggs. I prefer to buy my eggs directly from the farmer at the market. They're free-range and organic, and they taste better than regular eggs. But I alternate buying these eggs with the free-run organic eggs from the supermarket. The section for the free-run eggs is tiny – one row, maybe a dozen cartons, compared with a whole aisle of regular eggs from battery-cage hens. But if people don't buy them, the store will stop carrying them, so the only option will then be battery eggs. Sure, those "free-run" chickens never get to go outside. And like all poultry processors, the males are killed at birth since only the females are useful (this goes for the eggs available from the farmer as well, by the way, except in rare cases where the breed of chicken can also work as a meat bird, in which case the males may be raised and sold as capons). But they're still a step up from the regular eggs laid by chickens who live four to a square foot and go insane from the stress.

My point is about the message. By making an ethical (local, sustainable) purchase at the supermarket, we show the supermarkets that these are products that they should continue to carry because people are buying them. If the point in the "eat local" message is truly to support local farmers and ethical, sustainable businesses then we have to look at the bigger picture and do what we can to get everyone involved (and I don't mean just preaching at them). We can't do that if eating local is an elitist, rich person's domain.

True change only comes from bringing this movement to the masses and making it easy for them to access these products.

Last time I checked, the masses were buying their groceries at supermarkets.

# Cawfee

Coffee. Mud. Java. Cup o' Joe. Battery acid.

No matter what you call it, or how you drink it (black, double double, espresso), it's the Western world's most popular form of liquid fuel and energy.

I didn't actually start drinking coffee until I was 18 or so. Instead of a pot of coffee, my family has a constantly brewing pot of orange pekoe tea, sharp, bitter and acrid enough to strip the enamel off your teeth. To get it down, I drank it topped up with multiple spoonfuls of sugar, which probably also didn't help my dental work.

My first cup of coffee came when a boyfriend ordered one for me in a restaurant when I had gotten up to visit the restroom. "I drink tea!" I insisted upon my return. But coffee had always smelled so great... why not just try it? It took lots of sugar and cream, but I was hooked.

My first job in Toronto, the one I got the day after getting off the plane from Halifax because I realized how little money remained in my savings account, was at a chain coffee shop. Pre-Starbucks, Second Cup was a Canadian entity, and I scored a gig at one in the posh Forest Hill neighbourhood. Staffed by a motley assortment of punks, goths, hippie chicks and drag queens, much to the horror of the Chanel-suited locals, we'd all stop and do the Time Warp behind the counter as the song came on the local alternative radio station each afternoon around three o'clock.

It was the era of the flavoured coffee and we'd take turns flipping through the recipe book supplied by head office to create a variety of drinks made by combining the various flavours. Chocolate coffee + banana coffee + almond coffee = banana split coffee. These concoctions were various levels of awful, but they always seemed to sell out.

It was here that I learned how to pull a proper espresso, how to keep our hyper-active boss calm by slipping valium into his constantly topped up mug of brew, and how nobody needs to know that the tuna salad sandwiches are leftover from yesterday.

After chef's school, I returned to a gig at The Second Cup. Planning to open what would now be considered a "hipster" coffee shop (15 years before they started popping up in every funky neighbourhood), I figured I'd get a decent coffee education while making lattes and moccachinos for office workers. Instead, I found myself starting work at each morning at 5am to grind the day's beans, and using my culinary education to make fruit platters to go with the custom coffee orders for meetings in the office towers above us.

My bosses had no interest in having me learn anything beyond what head office required of me, despite the coffee "university" programme they had in place to make us all coffee "experts". Among the staff, however, I became the de facto assistant manager when the owner was gone, if only because of one occasion where someone had turned off the fountain drink machine over the Labour Day long weekend and we arrived back after three days to discover that the iced tea (made with a sugar-based mix) had grown a thick layer of mold across the top. Boss lady simply skimmed off the mold and turned the machine back on, while the rest of us stood gap-jawed at the thought of all the health and sanitation laws she was breaking, not to mention the risk she posed to customers.

"Don't sell the iced tea," was the refrain passed down the line, and in the morning rush, the part-time girls did their best to talk people out of a nice cold cup of upset stomach. As soon as boss lady had gone to a meeting, we drained that machine and scrubbed it down, taking turns keeping watch for her imminent return. If we had been caught it would have come down on my head – I'd have admitted to giving the order – and to cover their own butts, no doubt my co-workers would have thrown me under the bus.

Fortunately, we got the fresh batch made before she came back and kept the customers from buying any in the interim. But from that point on, I saw too many things that made me uncomfortable about the health and safety violations of the place and quit a few weeks later.

I suppose I should have narked her out, called head office or the health inspector, but I just wanted to be gone from the place, chalking up the experience to yet another example of how corporations and I don't work well together.

Which, in a roundabout way, is how I came to roast my own coffee.

I came across a display from Merchants of Green Coffee at an environmental fair in 2004 or so. The counter-top roaster was a cute thing, about the size of a popcorn maker, and the coffee it created was bright and fresh. Being able to roast it to the exact darkness I liked was a bonus, and Greg and I became early adopters of the home roasting process.

In the early days, the company delivered a batch of green beans each month via bicycle courier, and their ethos of fair trade and sustainably grown products jibed with our move to eating organic food and supporting small producers.

Roasting coffee at home is easy, but it makes a lot of smoke. I would actually set up the roaster on a wide outside window sill to keep the kitchen from filling with the oily smoke that would coat every surface, bits of loose chaff from the outside of the beans sticking to the grease like flaky scabs. This system worked until the winter, when the kitchen windows would freeze shut or when I'd have to brush a few inches of snow off the sill to keep the roaster stable. And then the outside temperature would mess with the temperature gauge on the roaster and the beans would brown unevenly.

It was a bit of an epiphany when I realized that the exhaust hood on my stove would do a decent job, although cleaning the coffee grease from the hood was an unpleasant task.

When we moved to an apartment, we started having problems. The exhaust fan in our kitchen does a terrible job. It does little to clear the room of smoke or steam, and we almost never cook meat or fish on top of the stove because the fan is so crap that the smoke detector – way at the other end of the apartment – will go off. Instead, we rigged up a large window fan set to exhaust and sent the smell of roasting coffee beans out into the world, hoping it would make our neighbours crave the stuff and not curse us for stinking up their homes.

When the roaster died after five years of regular use, as small appliances are wont to do these days, being mostly made from plastic, we replaced it with another just like it. Turns out, the market for home coffee roasters is pretty small and you really have to go up to the 500 dollar mark or so to get something solid. Our little 100 dollar roaster, while supposedly the same model as the first one, never really got the beans dark enough. What should have taken five to seven minutes took about fifteen and then never really got the beans past a medium roast.

We sought out beans from Papua New Guinea with notes of blackberries, Sumatra with chocolately undertones, or the many regions of Ethiopia, where the coffee is considered to be some of the best in the world in terms of flavour. All varieties that could take a dark roast. But the roaster just wasn't up to the job.

I had read about people roasting coffee in the oven, or in a popcorn popper (I tried this and it was an epic fail, it worked fine for a light roast but by the time the beans were roasted to our liking the clear plastic hood on the popper had started to melt, a sad, oozing howl of failure that taunts me to this day whenever I make popcorn). In Ethiopian restaurants, I noticed that they roasted coffee in an open frying pan, the server carrying the beans around the room as part of the coffee ceremony, filling the restaurant with the heady smell of smoke and chocolate and heaven, so I figured I'd give this method a try.

The trick to roasting coffee beans is to keep them moving all the time to ensure an even roast. Failure to do so can result in beans that are black and blistered on one side and still green on the other. Because the beans get super-hot, I used a frying pan with a glass lid to keep an eye on the colour while still being able to flip the beans and keep them moving.

This "cowboy" method of roasting coffee (how do you think they did it in pioneer days?) was reasonably effective, but required a lot of concentration. Unlike the roaster which had a cool-down phase, once my beans were the right colour – which would be just as they were making a cracking noise for the second time and starting to emit oil – I had to pull them off the heat and dump them into a sieve that was balanced atop a bowl. Leaving them in the pan, or even just dumping them into a bowl, would allow them to continue to cook, and ultimately burn.

The chaff-like skin that came off the beans as they roasted had a tendency either to stick to the lid of the frying pan or to flutter around the kitchen like tiny beige feathers that found their way into every corner and crevice.

Since I often forgot to roast the morning beans in advance, I would find myself juggling hot frying pans, sieves, oven mitts, and glass lids, a flurry of chaff swirling around me, all while bleary-eyed and half asleep. I needed a cup of coffee before I set about roasting more of the stuff. And there was really no way of ever getting around the smoke.

Fortunately, in the years when I had been diligently roasting my own coffee beans, many small companies had popped up selling locally roasted beans. Most focused on selling sustainable, fair trade, and organic coffee and made a point of working directly with farmers to bring them the best price and customers the best selection, and I am happy to give them my business.

There are times when I miss the excitement of watching the beans dance around the glass roasting chamber, expanding, cracking and transforming from a green seed to a black bean, emitting oil and the heady scent of the place it came from. But most mornings I am content to simply grind the beans that have been roasted by someone else and curse that old boyfriend for setting me on the path of delicious addiction.

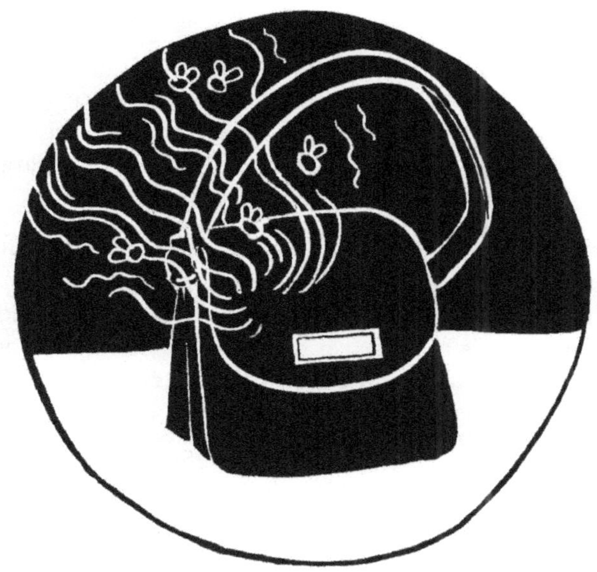

# Foie Gras Faux Pas

Every year we buy a food-related calendar for the kitchen. I'm not sure why, in this age of personal electronic devices, wall calendars are pretty much obsolete, and the selection becomes more and more sparse each year. But we have this one section of wall that needs something, and it's kind of fun to mark the passing of the months by flipping the page and enjoying a new picture for thirty days.

This year, our kitchen calendar is a collection of vintage food ads. None of them is exceptionally remarkable, but they meet the criteria of being food-related and vaguely retro. Like most calendars, we don't really look at the pictures as "art"; that is, we just enjoy the image and don't really analyze it too much.

On New Year's Day, we opened up the new calendar and flipped it open to January, where the ad is for a brand of foie gras: Edouard

Artzner of Strasbourg, France, a company that has been around since 1803.

First off, it's a bit risky including a foie gras ad in a food calendar – foie is the one food item that can start an argument faster than anything else I know – even some dedicated carnivores disapprove of it. But the ad itself is a source of great amusement.

A portly man is seated at a table on which is placed a half-full glass of wine or sherry and a lidded pot of foie gras, the lid removed to show that some has been consumed. The man is red in the face and appears to be asleep, his hands folded over his belly in a display of comfort and sophonsification. On each of the man's shoulders is a large white duck, their bills close together as if in conversation.

Here's the disturbing bit: we can't for the life of us figure out if the ducks are there to symbolize some sort of joy at the delicious repast, or if they're plotting the fat man's gruesome death as they peck his face off for eating their brother George.

It looks as if it's supposed to be a pleasant image, but really, it could well be a scene of impending carnage.

It took me many years to learn to like foie gras. My first impression, based on a mousse, was that it was not unlike liver-flavoured shortening.

I was at a restaurant opening once where the chef piped a foie gras mousse into cone shapes and then dipped them in chocolate and served them on a stick, similar to the classic chocolate-dipped cone from an ice cream truck. Figuring the chocolate would overpower the foie, I happily took one, only to immediately realize it was disgusting to me, and spit it out into a napkin. As it was a cocktail-style event, I was left with a paper napkin full of nasty foie and no place to put it. I didn't want to just leave it somewhere for someone else to come across and I couldn't find a server who could discretely take it away.

So I did what every other woman would do in the same situation – I balled up the napkin and shoved it in my purse. I'm not a fan of those granny purses with the million compartments, but this purse had a little side pocket, designed to hold a cell phone. Thinking that I didn't want to keep sticking my hand in ooky foie gras every time I went digging for a business card or my lipstick, I jammed the napkin in the pocket and zipped it shut.

Four days later when I pulled that bag out of the cabinet where I keep my purse collection, the stench was over powering. Fortunately the bag was washable, because let me tell you, there really is no other way to get the smell of rotting foie gras out of fabric.

Despite these bad experiences, I eventually grew to enjoy, if not love, foie gras. The turning point was one year on my husband's birthday. We were at a local restaurant that specializes in dishes prepared with beer, when the chef, who my husband knew, brought us a complimentary dish of foie gras cured in Belgian beer. I don't know if it was the flavour of the beer that did it, or if it was the simple preparation allowing the foie to remain in a firmer, more natural condition, but to date, it remains my favourite foie gras experience.

It would be remiss to write about foie gras and not discuss the ethical issues surrounding the product. But honestly, I can claim no expertise. There are as many people who defend the practice and list off all the reasons why it's sustainable and ethical as there are people who think its a cruel form of animal abuse. I'm not typically a fence-sitter, but I think both sides of the argument have merit. And as someone who thinks almost all industrial meat is cruel in various ways, to me it seems no different than how we treat other forms of poultry or pigs or cows.

Thankfully, between the number of people who don't like it, think it to be morally wrong, or flat out can't afford the stuff, foie gras doesn't really run the risk of ever going mainstream, which means that if the force-feeding required to create the fattened liver is cruel and painful to the birds, it's some small consolation to know that their number is smaller than it could be if more people ate the stuff.

And who knows? Maybe, someday, when we're least expecting it, the ducks will have their revenge.

# How Fortunate I Am

There is a fairly standard reaction amongst people when you tell them you're a food writer.

"Oh, I wish I had YOUR job!" they'll gush, picturing themselves seated at a table in a high-end restaurant, battalions of servers delivering domed silver trays of lobster, steak, and oysters – all for free of course – an array of wine glasses lined up before them.

This is about as far as the fantasy develops, and they never want to hear about the truly bad meals, the weight gain, the ulcers, or the various forms of digestive upset that come from eating too much. Or the food poisoning. They really don't want to hear about the food poisoning.

They certainly don't want to hear about the process of sitting down to write, of putting the experience into coherent thoughts that can be shared with others. And they're nothing but bemused – surely you've got to be making it up – when they're told about chefs stalking writers who have given a bad review, or the array of trolling comments left on an online article or blog post (oddly all from gmail accounts).

No, most people, when they think of food writing, never make it past the part where they get to eat the tasty free food.

And, okay, sure, there's plenty of that. There's even a fair amount of it that's free. The number of media events, openings, and tasting events seems to have multiplied in the five years or so since I started writing about food in this city, and I actually took a break from writing about the local restaurant scene recently because it all started to blend together.

That catfish breaded with pumpernickel crumbs and served with pickled egg white – did I have that at Acadia or URSA? How many restaurants are now taking part in the (more than) Group of 7 Chefs dining events? When is that new restaurant with the Peruvian and Persian fusion cuisine supposed to open?

I knew I had to stop when I couldn't remember what I had eaten the night before. Even with visual aids. Like any good food blogger, I went out to dinner with my camera in tow, trying not to be obnoxious, but regularly screeching at friends not to touch their food before I could get a photo of it. These photos served a purpose beyond sheer internet food porn. Looking at the images of my dinner from the night before, I was, for a long time, able to relive it in my head the next day as I was writing about it. To the point that I seldom took many notes about ingredients – if I could identify it, I could remember it.

I'd sort through the photos the next day, and just looking at the image would bring back the flavours and textures and smells of the dish. I could capture the nuances of spices, the aromatics of a smoking process; it was as if the dish sat before me again in real life. (I should probably note that I have a type of synesthesia, wherein senses cross over – the letter E, for instance, is always green – which tended to make tasting events, particularly with wine, bizarrely interesting, mostly due to my sweeping pronouncements along the lines of "This wine tastes like San Francisco on a cloudy day." Not everybody got where I was coming from.)

In any case, one day it stopped. The process didn't work any more. I had been writing about food for six years straight at that point, initially covering food politics and nutrition, then moving into the local food scene and then writing specifically restaurant news. I was burnt out, in a big way, and both my palate and my memory rebelled.

Despite the idea of being out of the loop, of not getting the great invites to the great events, of missing out on all the new places that were opening, too many to hit them all, I stopped. I settled in to write this book, and with a few exceptions including my local pub, and the neighbourhood Vietnamese pho joint, I stopped eating out.

I cooked, oh I cooked. Covering restaurants meant eating out at least three or four nights a week, and not doing that meant that I got to prepare my own food for the first time in a long while. Simple dishes – roast chicken, lasagna, pots and pots of lovely soups – all helped me to remember that I loved cooking as much as I loved eating.

But this piece isn't about my home cooking. Or taking a break to write. It's about how truly grateful I am to be at the point where I have enough experiences under my belt to be able to write a book about my food adventures. Most of these opportunities were the result of restaurants, or PR companies, or businesses wanting coverage, and most of them, if they were specific to Toronto, I wrote about on TasteTO. Many of the things I was invited to take part in were not open to the public, such as various tastings or media dinners. And some were just utterly outrageous.

Dinner in the Sky is an event service based in France where guests are strapped in to seats around a giant table and are hoisted up to 50 metres in the air to enjoy a meal while literally looking down on people. When it came to Toronto on a publicity junket, I was offered a pair of seats at a dinner. The food wasn't fantastic, but dangling for an hour above Toronto's Yonge Dundas Square was definitely a thrill.

Also a thrill, but of a distinctly different flavour, was the opportunity to travel with the staff from the Gladstone Hotel to the CSA farm they partner with and spend a day working in the fields. All I did was weed some rows of peas, but the lunch we all shared in the barn, dogs and chickens wandering around us, with dark thunderclouds forming as an impending storm rolled in across the acres of fields, was one of the best meals I've ever eaten. Yes, it was mostly just salad and peas and some ham from a recently slaughtered pig, but it was such a convivial meal, all of us tired and sun-kissed, hay crunching underfoot, that it remains one of my most beloved experiences as a food writer.

I also had the opportunity to judge some contests along the way. In 2011, I judged a gefilte fish contest at Caplansky's Deli, and learned a lot in the process (I may be one of the few people who actually like the traditional Jewish dish), and as part of Toronto Beer Week, I was also lucky enough to be a judge for a sticky toffee pudding contest at a pub called Monk's Table. And lest readers start thinking "I wish I had your job!", remember that one serving of sticky toffee pudding is a joy; a rich buttery sauce over a moist, date-studded cake. Four servings, with beer pairings, gets to be a little much by the end of it all.

There were also the events where I'd have to pinch myself at my great fortune. Times when my husband, Greg, and I would survey the company we had been included with, look at each other and mouth the words, "How the hell did we get here?"

When we were just starting out, an invite to a luncheon at a posh restaurant called The Fifth for a book by a Vancouver chef had us rubbing elbows with some of the most respected food writers in the country – people who were household names from newspapers and magazines, who had been established in their careers for years. It was incredibly flattering, us with our little blog, to be included with Toronto's food literati. That luncheon went on forever, the wine glasses were never empty, and we headed home with not just a buzz of excitement but a blood alcohol level so high we both sat on the sofa and let the living room spin around us.

On another occasion, and I'm still not sure how I warranted an invite, I sat in the dining room of the model suite for the posh condos that were to be part of the new Four Seasons Hotel and ate lunch with Chef Daniel Boulud and a handful of other journalists. At the time, I didn't even have anywhere to write about it (I was writing for the Toronto Star's entertainment website, but the paper's food editor, Jennifer Bain, was actually interviewing Boulud for a feature so I couldn't cover the event), but there I was, trying not to make a fool of myself surrounded by the chef, some hotel executives, and TV host Ben Mulroney.

It's also an ongoing joke between Greg and me that, at any event promoting food products from another country, I will always end up seated next to the ambassador, consulate-general, or princess from said country. It happened at a dinner promoting a Czech beer, at a dinner hosted by the Korean consulate, and at an event where a chef from Argentina did a guest stint at a local hotel. I don't travel much, so the question, "Have you been to my country?" is almost always an awkward one. I don't assume these folks care much about how I fear getting on a plane because of my perfume allergy.

And the food, oh the food. Yes, I have eaten some outstanding food over the past few years. We joke that our dog is the only one in the city who regularly gets table scraps of foie gras, steak, and lobster because we're always coming home with doggy bags from some posh dinner or event.

Some of the most memorable items include civet cat coffee with Derek Zavislake from Merchants of Green Coffee (yes, that's the stuff the civet cats eat and poop out again). It was dusky and smoky and almost burned the back of the throat; interesting, but I'm not sure I'd pay top dollar for it.

At a wine event at the Royal York Hotel, where the food stations included an oyster bar, I ate 25 of the things before Greg cut me off, fearful that I'd get sick. There was so much food that, unbelievably, the oyster bar was empty of guests, and as I tipped back one after the other, the shucker delighted in telling me about the providence of each variety. I slurped their briny sweetness, eschewing lemon, horseradish and hot sauce in favour of the nuances of each type. That was a wonderfully good night.

On another occasion, Greg, who writes about beer and spirits, was invited to a whisky dinner at an renowned and extremely high-end steak house. It was the kind of place that we'd never normally go, even in our quest to check out great restaurants on our own dime, just to be familiar with what they do and to enjoy a fantastic meal. The premise was a media preview for a tie-in between a famous whisky and Father's Day, where guests were encouraged to bring "a man that they admire". Greg brought me instead. We sat with another local booze writer and the friend she had brought along. The food was posh but not outstanding until we got to the steak, a rib-eye that had to have been 3 inches thick. Cooked to a doneness barely past rare, it was charred on the outside and still oozing pinkness on the inside. And it didn't go with the whisky at all.

The friend of the drink writer called our server over and ordered us all glasses of a Spanish Rioja. It was a bold thing to do; the wine would undoubtedly go on the PR company's tab, likely with a mark-up, but as we sat there with huge wine glasses and shit-eating grins, we all agreed that the wine, with its leathery tobacco notes, was a much better pairing with the fantastic steaks. We were officially the rowdy table that night, but it was one of the best events I've been to, simply because the company was so delightful.

Sometimes the events we attended were just odd. We spent an afternoon in a hotel conference room sampling olive oils from the various regions of Argentina. Grassy, spicy, sweet, acidic – I had no idea that olive oil was so diverse. Or so very good for the digestion. Go on, drink about half a cup of olive oil (which is what all of our many samples added up to) and see what results you get.

There were, of course, many outstanding dinners. Local Chef Matt Kantor's El Bulli dinner that he presented in the middle of The Cookbook Store was 20-plus courses of fun, from the hot frozen gin fizz, crackers made with olives, parmesan marshmallows and foie gras mousse which so closely resembled a wedge of sponge toffee on our plates that the table uttered a collective "Ohhh!" as the foie melted on our tongues.

And on the theme of molecular gastronomy, Chef Thorarinn Eggertsson of Orange in Reykjavik, Iceland, did a stint at The Drake

Hotel where he served up reindeer, langoustines and frozen chocolate mousse in the shape of a rubber duck, vanilla sauce mixed with liquid nitrogen (for the bubbles) and a pineapple sauce served in a hand soap dispenser. I enjoyed this meal so much at the media preview that I returned with Greg to eat it again.

On another occasion, we were the guests of Oceanwise, an organization that promotes sustainable seafood in restaurants across the country. After cocktails and an amuse bouche at the Royal York Hotel, media were loaded into vans for a roving (secret) dinner to sample sustainable fish dishes at local restaurants. There were shouts of excitement as our driver pulled up in front of noted restaurants Scaramouche, where we had exquisite scallops; Pangaea, for seared Pacific cod; and then to end the night, The Harbord Room for another cod dish.

When I started writing, I considered myself shy. I had a hard time talking to strangers. I am still far more of an introvert than an extrovert (I think that's the case with most writers: we dig our quiet time), but between the many media events and the popularity of pop-up dinners around Toronto, I am happily now quite comfortable eating with, and talking to, strangers. I still aim for a seat at the end of the table – there's that pesky perfume allergy to take into account, and being left-handed makes for some jostling difficulties when the seating is tight – but I can hold my own. And I've met some fantastic and truly interesting people. I've eaten foie gras in a can from Montreal restaurant Au Pied Du Cochon in a Toronto art gallery. I've enjoyed Chef Ben Heaton's gorgeous British cuisine at a pop-up in a wood shop as a promotion for his restaurant The Grove, and I've had some truly memorable evenings around the table at The Rusholme Park Supper Club, a BYOB dinner series where local chefs work with owner Len Senater to create one-off dinners on a variety of themes.

There's more, of course. Too much to list, although I wish I could thank every chef, restaurateur, farmer, food artisan, and PR person who let me into their kitchen, put plates of food in front of me, invited me to events or supported what we've done over the years. To say that I appreciate their help, their hospitality, would be a huge understatement.

It's not a perfect industry. As fantastic as the local food scene is, we're not all one big happy family. There are rivalries, competitions, business deals gone sour, chefs who take advantage of their staff, and staff who don't live up to their potential. On the writing side of things, just as in the kitchen, creativity can equal eccentric (and not in a good way), so disagreements over work can quickly turn to bad blood with writers blaming editors and editors blaming writers, and plenty of shit-talking on each side.

There's also an uneasiness between chefs and food writers, particularly critics, and especially bloggers, who might not know as much about the food they're writing about as they should. I don't know that we'll ever achieve some kind of armistice, some truce or level of peace where the two sides actually work together for the overall good. The food industry is one of unique personalities, many of whom live, work, play – and fight – hard.

I've exerted great effort not to make this final piece appear as if I'm bragging. "Look at me, eating the free foie gras!" Certainly, there are others in the industry who get more freebies, more invites, more extra plates of stuff that never appear on the final bill than I do. And I don't want to reinforce the idea that the job is all about the fun stuff. As I make clear, it's very hard work.

I'm not religious, so the term "blessed" doesn't really get much use in my vocabulary. Lucky, maybe; fortunate, definitely. Appreciative, thankful, grateful – all of these. To have had the opportunities these past few years, to be able to tell the food stories of my city, to be able to share news, or tips, or tell readers about some fantastic new place, and then revel in that restaurant's success because I so love what they're doing... it's an honour. I couldn't be more proud if someone was pinning a medal to my chest.

Sitting at a dinner, touring a chef's kitchen, or being greeted by a wandering flock of chickens on a farm, my heart bursts with pride, thankfulness, and joy. There's always just a little bit of trepidation left over from that shy girl I was when I started all this – the vein of worry and fear, always there, no matter how confident I may appear on the outside, that comes with the responsibility of telling people's stories in a way that is honest, fair and authentic. When people put up their life savings, or mortgage their house, in order to fulfil their life's dream and start a restaurant, you want to do right by them.

To have had the opportunity to do that, to have been accepted and welcomed, and lauded for my work – is worth more to me than everything else. Yes, it's a damned great job, but not for the reasons people think. It's a damned great job because when everything falls into place, it means being a part of something big - the promotion of the local dining scene as a whole, but also of something small – the individual stories within the bigger machine.

Life hasn't always turned out smoothly these past few years; there have been bumps along the way. But when I look back at my place in the Toronto food scene, and at the work that I've done, and the people I've had the opportunity to meet, and work with, and write about, I wouldn't change a thing.

# Acknowledgements

Self-publishing is a lonely and often frustrating endeavour, and during the process of putting this book together, I regularly said that the writing was actually the easy part. So thanks go – first and foremost – to my dog Tula, who was with me through the stress of ISBN numbers, bar codes, widowed text, and em dashes, and sat by my side offering a head to pat and an ear to scratch when my page layout changed on its own. She never had any great advice, and she never offered to help fix any of it, but she listened without judgement when I needed to rant.

Big huge thanks to Katherine Verhoeven who made the book oh so beautiful with her fun and fabulous illustrations. She is crazy talented and I am so happy to have had the opportunity to work with her.

Also, my unwavering appreciation and devotion and respect and thanks to Jodi Lewchuk who was just going to "read over" my text and instead gave me a full editing job – most of which I proceeded (probably out of my own stupidity) to ignore, because I'm rebellious like that. All errors within this book probably occurred because Jodi pointed them out and I went, "Screw you, Chicago style guide! I'm doing it MY way!"

Thanks as well to my husband Greg and my family, immediate and extended, as well as friends throughout the years, without whom these stories could not have happened.

www.ingramcontent.com/pod-product-compliance
Lightning Source LLC
Chambersburg PA
CBHW021058090426
42738CB00006B/400
*9780991737703*